Real Life Stories

Compiled by
EJ Thornton &
Capri Brock

Books To Believe In
Copyright 2013

A Books to Believe In Publication
All Rights Reserved
Copyright 2013 by Great Angel Books

Books To Believe In
www.BooksToBelieveIn.com
www.Getting-Published.com

17011 Lincoln Ave. #408
Parker, CO 80134

Phone: (303) 794-8888
Fax: (720) 863-2013

www.GreatAngelBooks.com

Foreword

by EJ Thornton

Angel On Board is a very special book. It is a fictionalized version of real events. Many of the angel stories in *Angel On Board* really did happen. Many fans have asked EJ to recount the real stories because they are also quite fascinating.

Angels have always been around EJ and her family and so there are even more real-life angel stories that EJ and her family have experienced.

Once *Angel On Board* became the sensation it did, EJ started receiving letters about other people's angels and their stories. So we have decided to share those with our readers as well.

We would like to keep this series going, so at the back of the book, we will point you to the place where you can share your amazing Angel stories and they can be in a future version of *Angel On Board—Real Life Stories!*

Angel On Board—Real Life Stories is 11 years in the making. I recently found the first request I ever wrote to someone asking them for their angel story dated 6/1/2001.

One of the authors working with me named Sue Scudder (medium and author of The Voice Across the Veil) had been able to reach my late brother John and he had a couple of messages for me. The first was that he loved me. The second was that I could always recognize him in the sarcasm.' John loved good sarcasm in life, so that fits. If there was good pun, or an interesting way to say something, he was always there too! So, when Sue said, "Watch for John in the sarcasm," I knew just what she meant.

A little later the same day, an e-mail request came in from GreatAngelBooks.com asking to be notified when *Angel On Board—Real Life Stories* was finished. My husband and co-owner of Books To Believe In is the one who receives all the Internet correspondence and forwards these requests to the appropriate person. In this case, it was me. After he forwarded it on, he added, "Do you think you'll ever finish that book?"

I didn't think much of that at the time. It was a bit out of character for him to say something sarcastic like that, but I dismissed it at that point. It still stuck in my consciousness for a while. A few hours later I called him on it. I asked, "Why did you say something so snide and sarcastic to me."

"I didn't say that," he told me.

Both Capri Brock and I heard him say that to me. Then I remembered what Sue said, "Watch for John in the sarcasm."

I wondered if I should make writing and collecting the *Angel On Board—Real Life Stories* a new priority. So I put the wheels in motion. I asked Capri Brock to help me collect the stories and collaborate with me on the book and she agreed. We started to organize what we had and made a list of what we still had to do.

The next morning, I opened my computer case and there was a stapled mass of papers in there that I had worked on many years prior. It was the last printing of *Angel On Board—Real Life Stories* . It contained about 6 stories and had red editing marks all over it. I recognized it instantly, although I hadn't see it for several years. Suddenly, it was in plain sight on top of my computer INSIDE my computer case? Another sign I surmised and went to work on the project in earnest!

I had worked on editing, writing and rewriting stories for most of that day and late into that night. I thought to myself, I would sure like a little validation that this is what I should be working on. So, I looked at the up-to-the-minute sales figures on Kindle. The Kindle version of *Angel On Board* hadn't sold any new copies that day. However, I saw the paperback version of *Angel On Board* had sold and the new sales rank was 117171.

My husband's favorite number is 17 and mine is 11. So, I thought the number was a good sign. But I took it one step further to see if Doreen Virtue's *Angel Numbers* had something to say to us about the 1's and 7's in combination. This is what her website said:

(http://spiritlibrary.com/doreen-virtue/number-sequences-from-the-angels)

1's and 7's, such as 117 or 771—This is confirmation that you are doing great. You are on the right path, so keep going! This is a sign that you have chosen your thoughts well and that you should focus more steadily on your objectives. Be sure to add appropriate emotions to your thoughts; for instance, feeling grateful for the gifts you have in life.

Gratitude will speed the process of your manifestations.

Truth is stranger than fiction and these stories are amazing! **#TRUTHisSTRANGER**

I received the validation I needed. That is why *Angel On Board—Real Life Stories* is finally available for you to read and enjoy! Blessings...

This story and all the following stories are true.

Disclaimer

We are aware that some people do not believe it is biblically correct that people become angels. That is okay, we don't all need to agree.

Some of our angels, the ones in these stories are known to us. The word 'ghost' didn't seem to fit and since most come with messages, especially messages of love, by that definition—they are angels.

Table of Contents

Physical Proof

Asking for Signs

Birds & Other Winged Creatures

Peace at Last

Incredible Coincidences

*Coincidences are just God's
way of remaining anonymous...*

~*Albert Einstein*

Bulldogs & Babies

by Capri Brock

Most people say that what my family and I went through in one day most people don't go through in a lifetime.

It was June 11th, 1989 and about eleven o'clock at night, our pregnant English Bulldog Shelby started showing signs of going into labor. This significantly miffed my mother, who not only was also pregnant, but she was 4 days overdue! My mom was due on June 7th, and my dog wasn't going to be due until June 14th. They thought it would have been plenty of time to get adjusted to a new baby before the puppies arrived.

Even though I was only three years old, my mom let me stay up with her to help take care of the dog, because she couldn't bend over very well and my father was gone, because he worked nights. He was due home about 3am.

I don't know if it was all the activity or just the power of suggestion, but by the time my dad had gotten home, my mother had also gone into labor as well. He was met at the door with pretty awesome news... to which he said, "Do I have time to take a nap?"

My mom let him go lay down for a little bit, because she had to take care of some things, like calling my aunt to come pick me up and get the hospital stuff all packed.

My aunt came to pick me up around 5am.

My mom's contractions were getting worse. It was clear, she couldn't stay to help with the birth of the puppies like they had planned. In fact, they were going to have to take the dog somewhere, because English Bulldog mothers have been known to roll over on their own puppies and not know it. They must be watched. So somewhere around 6am, my father drove my pregnant mother and our pregnant dog—both in labor—to their respective hospitals with the same car ride. My dad used to joke that he wanted to be pulled over, because he WANTED to tell this story to the judge!

They arrived at the animal hospital first. My mom was certain she had more time than the dog did, so she instructed my dad to take the dog first. Which he did. As my dad ushered the dog to the back of the vet's office, my mom filled out the paperwork and after a couple of choruses of "HeHeWho," the staff at the animal clinic assured her, "We deliver puppies not babies—we will remember you!"

Then they informed my dad that the clinic would be closing at 8am and he'd have to have the dog and puppies out by then. He looked at them in anguish and said, "I'll be a little busy."

It was the days way before cell phones, and my dad didn't expect to have to call anyone, so he didn't have his phone book with him. Somehow he had to get hold of the sire's owners and plea for help, which he somehow accomplished. So Shelby and the puppies were going to be taken care of, which was good. We found out later that Shelby started having the puppies about 1/2 hour after arrival and had two of them by 8am. The sire's owner transferred them to his vet where she had two more by about 9am.

My dad got my mom to the hospital about 8:30 and by 9:30, she was in the O.R. having an emergency c-Section. So, by 9:30, all the babies had been born!

Pediatricians have to be present for c-Sections, so my Pediatrician was in attendance for the birth of my sister.

I was at my Aunt Sylvia's house. I was overly excited because I knew that there was something major going on, but couldn't really comprehend everything. During the morning, I played with my cousins. They had a very old collie named Princess. I (obviously) had a dog of my own, so I was used to playing with dogs.I was too young to understand that old dogs played differently than younger dogs and sometimes they didn't want to play at all! I went to go pet their dog Princess. I stepped on her paw by accident; she bit me in my face right under my left eye. Freaked out, my aunt rushed me to the doctor to get my face looked at.

Luckily, my grandparents had unexpectedly showed up two days early because they wanted to help with the new baby, and when no one was at our house, they came to Aunt Sylvia's house. My aunt left her kids with them.

My aunt didn't want anyone else to tell my mom what had happened to me. She figured that my mom had enough to deal with other than worrying about me, so we all swore not to say a word my mom about my dog bite—until of course, I went to the hospital and she could see the damage first-hand.

Not a perfect plan...

The Doctor came into the exam room and looked at the chart and announced, "I was just delivering a baby with the last name of Brock, when I got the page back to the office."

I proudly announced that was my sister!

"Wow!" was all she had to say. She didn't even know about the Bulldogs!

There wasn't any permanent damage, but I did receive two

stitches.

It was about 3pm and my mom wanted to know where I was because she wanted to introduce my to my baby sister. She was still none-the-wiser about the dog bite, but she knew something was going on. My grandma went to visit her in the hospital without me. Mom started to question her about my whereabouts. Even after the affects of anesthesia, my mom caught Grandma in a slip-up, so Grandma was forced to tell her what had happened to me.

I was brought up to the room and out of everything that happened that day I do remember every detail about that moment. I was holding my dad's hand, standing in the doorway. I was all dressed up in my little overall dress and pink and purple striped shirt and two little pig tails. I had to look good; after all I was a big sister now! I did the best I could with a big bandage on my face. I looked into the room and saw my mom on the bed holding my baby sister and smiling at me.

Shortly thereafter, I left to go home with my dad and grandparents to a house full of puppies!

What a great day.

In one day my family had five new family members. Three new baby girls and two new baby boys, one human, four puppies and one big sister with stitches under her eye.

The lesson learned from that day was that no matter how much planning goes into pregnancies, dog or human, they never come on time. If you're silly enough to plan two pregnancies due within a week of each other, you better be sure the angels will be working overtime keeping everyone and everything safe, but that's not to say they won't get some good laughs out of the whole deal!

Winter Blooms

by EJ Thornton

My brother John was killed suddenly on July 11, when he was just 31-years-old. He had just celebrated his second anniversary with his wife. They had a young 6 month old son. John adored his family.

On his second anniversary, exactly one week before he left this plane of existence, he gave his wife two small blooming house plants.

The next six months for his family were of course terrible and stressful. It was made even more stressful because his wife decided to move to Spokane Washington as well, to be closer to her family.

Still wanting John's son to have a joyful childhood and a normal life, we all celebrated the holidays and birthdays. The baby's first birthday was in the middle of winter. on January 10, one day before the six month anniversary of John's untimely death.

The plants that John gave his wife were treasured and kept in plain sight. Just a couple of days before the baby's birthday, they started to act as thought they were going to bloom—and that's exactly what they did on John's son's first birthday. The plants both bloomed in the middle of winter...

Even if they were winter blossoming plants, like Jade or amaryllis or paperwhites (they weren't), something very special had to have been encouraging them BOTH to bloom right on time. It was just John's way of saying, "Happy Birthday, son!"

More Blooms...

by John Craig

My wonderful wife of 34 years, Jeanie suddenly and unexpectedly passed away in August, 2005 of a burst brain aneurysm. Jeanie was a strong person, the kind who absolutely would continue to be present for her family, if there was any way possible. She was always full of life, with a passion for helping others and with a strength of character based on loving, strong, sheer will power. I loved her dearly, and I still do.

I have several stories of how Jeanie has managed to communicate across the veil, in one case even clearly saving my life. The story I want to share here though, is of an odd set of coincidences meant to signal to her extended family that she's still with us, communicating that message in one of those unfathomable ways that angels do.

A few short weeks before her passing, we camped once again in Yellowstone, one of Jeanie's favorite places to be. I hopped out of our car near the north entrance to the park to take a picture of the beautiful yellow flowers blooming that summer on the native cactus plants covering the ground. Jeanie liked those flowers, and I was determined to bring home a good close-up picture. Once the picture was snapped, I stood up to discover a cluster of long cactus needles sticking out of my leg, snagged by my skin once I knelt down. I pulled one or two of the 2-inch long needles out, but several more disappeared into my shin. The doctor at the local clinic dug around, but they are still in there somewhere to this day.

Upon returning home, the cactus pictures turned out to be very nice. For weeks we joked about those plants, and the price I'd paid to get that photo. Cactus plants and flowers were on our minds!

Then, suddenly, everything changed literally overnight. Jeanie was gone forever the morning I woke to discover her lifeless body. Within a few days we had a memorial service—it's all such a blur to me now in so many ways.

Not too long afterwards, Jeanie's sister Linda brought to my attention an interesting story, and a picture for me to hang on my wall forever. Linda's sister in law had a cactus plant in their home, a cactus that had never bloomed in the dozen or so years it was in their family.

On the afternoon of Jeanie's memorial service, it bloomed for the first and only time, with multiple flowers! Pictures were taken, they were framed nicely, and then presented to us.

For me, the cactus flowers' message had very special meaning, tying in perfectly with our last Yellowstone trip, a place Jeanie loved dearly. I know it was her way of telling her sister, and me, that all was okay, and that life goes on in mysterious but wonderful ways.

A Very Special Birthday Present

by John Craig

It was January 29, 2010 and I went out to the storage shed to look for something. I wasn't the last one in the shed, obviously, because a box had fallen over and it hadn't been cleaned up. I always clean up messes I make... if you don't believe me, ask my wife... well, maybe you better not.

All the same, a box of VHS video tapes had fallen and they were scattered all over the floor of the shed. Most had fallen in a heap, but one had distanced itself from the others and was sitting all by itself near the door of the shed, kinda like it wanted to get out.

I picked it up and read the date on it: January 29, 1998. Wow, I thought, what are the odds that I pick up a tape with today's date on it. Then I realized that 1998 was the year that my granddaughter Makayla was born and this was a video of her birth.

Jeanie and I were both present at Makayla's birth and there were many times on that video where Jeanie told an unborn and newborn Makayla how much she loved her. I stopped what I was doing and got Makayla and we watched the video. We both cried, but they were tears of remembrance and joy.

We're both pretty sure that Jeanie just wanted to have Makayla hear her personally tell her she loved her all over again. especially, on her birthday.

Belated Valentine

by John Craig & EJ Thornton

EJ wrote *Angel On Board*, a book where she says almost all the human' events happened, although she took some liberties with angelic events. It is a fiction book after all.

There is one scene in the book that is pure fiction, or at least it was fiction until it played out in real life many years after it was written.

The scene in the book is on the day of Martin's funeral when he re-gifts a Valentine card to his wife just to remind her how much he loves her. That part was fiction...

John lost Jeanie in August of 2005. EJ and John had been friends for 25 years prior. They worked together in the early 1980s. EJ knew and was very fond of Jeanie too. *Angel On Board's* ability to help the grieving was well documented, so EJ sent John a copy of the book and he swears that it really helped him cope with the loss of his beloved wife.

John had been finding things periodically that Jeanie hadn't put away or that she had stashed in a drawer or closet. When he'd find these old cards, notes or momentos, they'd usually take his breath away, because he'd just been missing her so much. It always seemed like she could find a way to remind him that she still loved him.

John was an author and he had a basement office which was purely his domain. The grandchildren knew better than to go in it and unless they were getting their laundry, they rarely ventured into the basement anyway. John and the grandkids were the only ones living in his house after Jeanie passed away.

It was just a couple of days after Valentine's day, February 19th to be exact, and when John went down to his basement office that day, there was a card on his computer desk that wasn't there the day before.

It was a Valentine's card from Jeanie, one dated February 19—five years prior. In the card, she wrote, "I'm sorry this is late."

John vaguely remembers receiving the card five years prior, and he did recognize it. What he didn't recognize though, was that inside the card was another card with a hand-written note from Jeanie saying how much she missed him.

How did the card get there? So far we haven't come up with an alternate plausible scenario, so we're just gonna go with Jeanie re-gifted him the Valentine's card and wrote a quick note to go along with it.

The Wizard and the Magazine

by EJ Thornton

As a publisher of many books, sometimes I would organize a group book signing event in conjunction with a local bookstore. If I could get 5 or more of my authors to agree to an event, then I'd get a store to book *"The League of Extraordinary Authors."*

I organized just such an event for a Saturday morning at the Southglenn Mall in Centennial Colorado several years ago. We had about 8 authors show up, from fiction authors, to poets, we had an eclectic bunch. I sat one of my non-fiction writers next to my 'wizard' - which proved an interesting match up. Glenn, my wizard, had fairy dust sprinkled all around his space on the table he shared with Jude, an author of a book on how to effectively deal with Chronic Pain. Glenn could also talk anyone's ear off, so he was a terrific addition to the panel of authors when there were customers about, but he only had Jude to talk to when there weren't.

I was sitting on the other side of the Jude and I felt my ankle get kicked, and Jude indicated as nonchalantly as she could that the enjoyment of sitting next to Glenn was waning.

So, I got up and went to the magazine rack in the bookstore. I stood there for a moment, picked up a special edition writing magazine called "Writer's Digest" and called Jude over.

"Thank you, thank you, thank you!" she whispered when Glenn was out of ear shot. "I didn't want to hurt his feelings, but I needed a quick break."

I said, "Well, to make this ruse work, you're going to have to buy this magazine or one just like it. Then you'll have something to read when you go back." Jude quickly grabbed the one I'd been holding and went to the cash register to purchase it.

I went back to the table. After browsing a few more things in the store. Jude returned to her seat next to Glenn, but now she had the magazine opened and was reading it.

After about 10 minutes, she backhanded my arm and said, "Now I know why you recommended THIS magazine! Why didn't you tell me?"

I was caught completely off guard. "Tell you what?" I asked.

"That your name is in this magazine!" Jude exclaimed.

Stunned at what she was saying, I took a look at what she was pointing at and there it was, my name and my company's name on a list of the Top Print-on-Demand Publishers in the USA.

I chose that magazine because I used it and I was fond of it. I was chosen to be on that same list a year prior, but I did not know that list would be published again, nor that the list was in the edition I grabbed off the shelf. Even the year before, when I was listed, I didn't know about it until someone called and told me that they had found my company's listing in the magazine.

If Jude hadn't have told me, I would have missed out completely knowing that my company had received such high praise! I don't know which of my author-angels might have been pulling the strings that day - but thanks!

Glenn now is among my author-angels, and I think of him when I see anything that sparkles like glitter.

Just Sayin' Hi

by EJ Thornton

I love those moments in life when you just have to sit back and calculate the odds of something happening. Then when you realize the odds are just too great to have that be a coincidence, you draw some true meaning from the moment.

Just about 6 months after my father Floyd passed away (remember <u>Bulldogs & Babies</u> and <u>The Invisible Hand</u>), I was taking a walk on the greenbelt near my house when a lady walking two white English Bulldogs were coming directly at me.

If any of you know the sub culture of English Bulldog owners, it is that everyone loves everyone else's dog and just has to go pet them. So, as they approached, I asked if I could pet her puppies. I started to pet the bigger one and I asked the name.

"Floyd," she answered.

I chuckled, "Of course it is," and smiled. "Hi Dad!"

The dog owner was a little confused until I explained, all the while petting a friendly bulldog named Floyd. We all wondered, "What are the odds?" Then we went our merry ways.

Little moments like that - sometimes can be very long-lasting memories. "Hi Floyd!"

Double Take

by Capri Brock

Like most, I had a routine while getting ready in the morning. It consisted of showering, doing my makeup, fixing my hair, getting dressed and then putting my jewelry on-which consisted of two rings and a necklace. Both of the rings were special, one was a family heirloom that my mom gave to me and the other was my commitment ring from my boyfriend. I wore both on their respected ring fingers. I never went anywhere without both of them on.

It was a normal day, I was up getting ready for work, going through the typical motions of the routine. I always take my rings off before I get into the shower. Television has taught us all that rings fall down drains and trying to retrieve them results in a flooded bathroom and A LOT of explaining to do.

I finished getting ready, then headed off to work. It wasn't until I was at work a few hours later that my heart dropped. I looked down at my hand and realized that I had only one of my rings on. I was missing my ring from my boyfriend.

There was a panic of emotions going through my head.

Where could I have lost it?

How would I go about finding it?

What if I lost it before I got to work?

How could it have fallen off my finger and I didn't notice?

Most of all, how was I going to tell my boyfriend, who I work with, that I had lost the ring he gave me?

After a few anguishing moments, I decided to tell my boyfriend what had happened. "Babe, I have something to tell you."

He saw that I was clearly shaken. "What is it honey?"

"I lost the ring that you gave me, I can't find it and I don't know what to do. I have my other ring on, so I know I didn't forget to put them on..."

I started rambling on and on. He, being a little more level-headed than I was at that moment, came up with a plan. We'd retrace my steps that day and ask if anyone else we worked with had seen the missing ring.

I got on the walkie-talkie and explained my situation, "Guys, I lost my ring. I can't find it. Will everyone keep an eye out for it for me today?"

My wonderful co-workers, who also were good friends, dropped what they were doing because a scavenger hunt sounded more exciting than actually working. We all started scouring the building and the surrounding area.

"Capri, what does the ring look like?" squawked the walkie.

"Where have you been in the building today?"

"Have you checked lost and found?"

"Maybe a guest has turned it in already."

After about twenty minutes of searching high and low, everyone returned empty-handed. I was in tears and decided that it was pointless to keep searching.

Disappointed, I collected myself, and returned back to work. I was organizing the aisles of shoes, trying to get through the rest of the day. I racked my brain as to where else I could look.

I tried to convince myself that it had to be at home; that was the only plausible solution. I hadn't been anywhere else that day.

Off in my thoughts, I snapped out of it when I heard my name over the walkie-talkie from my friend, Jay. "Capri, what did your ring look like?"

With a lump in my throat, I got on the walkie and described it again. "It is a white-gold ring, with two interlocking hearts, two diamonds in the centers of the hearts and 3 small diamonds in the band on either side of the hearts."

After what seemed like an eternity, Jay came back over the walkie and said, "We found it! We are outside on the side parking lot."

A few other co-workers and my boyfriend had to run to keep up with me as I dashed outside to meet them.

There it was-my white-gold ring, with two interlocking hearts, two diamonds in the centers of the hearts and 3 small diamonds in the band on either side of the hearts.

I hugged Jay and Jack for finding the impossible, it was probably the only time in my entire life I was thankful that someone took a smoke break. I couldn't believe my luck, they found my ring in the parking lot, where hundreds of cars drove through and just as many people walked. I promptly put it on my finger and returned to work. I proceeded to check my finger every two minutes for the rest of the day to ensure it was still there.

Once my adrenaline subsided, I examined the ring. It was somewhat worse for wear. It looked like a car had run over it. The prongs were smashed into the diamonds, and it also looked tarnished. I was sad that for the short amount of time it was off my finger, so much damage had been done to it. But I was elated that I had my ring back; I would do anything that I needed to do to fix it.

It felt like show-and-tell after that, with all of my concerned co-workers coming to find me to see the now-infamous ring.

"They really found the ring, they weren't just playing a joke on you?" asked one co-worker.

"Nope, I don't know how they found it, but they did. I can't believe it!" as I put out my hand for her to see the actual proof of the ring on my finger.

It was a few weeks later, life had returned back to normal. My mom and I decided that it was time to re-decorate the bathroom and give it a little face lift. I was in Interior Design school at the time, so I jumped at the opportunity to go buy new things for the house. I came up with an entire new concept for the bathroom. Once I had all the supplies in order, I was ready to get my project underway.

I started with the shower curtain. Now I have changed a shower curtain once or twice before, and I knew that I wasn't the tallest person, so I needed to stand on the toilet in order to change out the curtains. I had too much work to do, I had to avoid having my arms feel like dead weights just because of a silly shower curtain. I stood up on the toilet and something shiny caught my attention. Carefully, I climbed over the obstacles and reached the bathtub, to see what it was on the high ledge.

I couldn't believe it—there was my ring. If that was my ring, whose ring did I have on my hand and how could it be an exact duplicate?

I guess I screamed pretty loud, because my mom rushed to the bathroom to see if I was all right. When she got there she saw me, standing there holding my ring in my hand.

"Capri, are you ok? What is wrong?"

"I, I..." Before I could really form words, I threw up my hand which had my ring' on it. However, I was holding my actual ring.

"What the...Wait, Oh my God, is that your ring?" she was astonished at the sight of two duplicate rings.

"Yes, THIS is my ring!" I pointed to the one in my hand.

"But the one on your hand is the one you found in the parking lot at work, right?" she asked confused.

"Yes..." I still couldn't come up with much to say at that point. I kept asking myself if this was real.

Was I being set up, was this a big joke?

No, no... I dismissed this thought quickly; too much planning and money would have had to go into this prank, if this was truly a set up.

I called my boyfriend, asked him to come over and I showed him the ring I had found in the bathroom. He was just as astonished as I was.

"No, Babe, I wouldn't play a trick on you like that. Something else, maybe, but I wouldn't play around with your ring," he reassured me.

Piecing together the mystery, what had happened was, I had taken off my mom's ring before I got into the shower that day, but I hadn't taken off my boyfriend's ring. Once I realized that, I wanted to avoid the "down the drain" fiasco that I knew would come from wearing jewelry in the shower, so I slipped that ring off and placed it on the ledge above my head, back far enough so it wouldn't drop—and just enough out of my line of sight to not see it. I had to get up really early that day, so I just didn't remember doing that. Placing the ring there slipped my mind after I got out of the shower and my auto-routine kicked back in. It didn't register that I only had one ring on. So, I finished getting ready for the work day and left.

The day after I found my real ring, I had to work again. And I knew what I had to do. I would have to turn the parking lot' ring into lost and found. There was someone else out there who lost their ring. I knew what the ring meant to me and how I felt when I thought that it was lost, never to be seen again. I also knew the relief and joy that I felt after I got it back. If I could give that same relief and joy back to whoever lost their ring in the parking lot, I wanted to do that.

I also knew that I would have to be ready to tell all of my co-workers the next installment of the story of my ring.

I got to work, turned in the ring to lost and found. The store policy at work was, after 30 days if no one had claimed what was turned in, it went to the person that turned it in.

"Are you going to come back and get the ring if no one claims it?" asked one of my friends.

"I don't know, probably...it would be cool to have two of the same rings." I said.

"Good insurance plan, if you ever lose one ring you have a backup for next time," she said.

I laughed thinking of what my boyfriend would think, if he had heard that comment.

After 30 days and a constant reminder from my co-workers-who were just as intrigued, I went back to the lost and found to see if the mysterious 2nd ring was still there or if it's true owner had shown up to claim it.

The ring was still there, no one had claimed it. As excited as I was that I could keep it and now have an insurance plan if I was to ever lose the ring again, I was a little saddened that the other owner never got their ring back. But, I couldn't just leave it in the lost and found after everything that had happened. I took the ring home and placed it safely in my jewelry box.

One day—probably with the help of a master mathematician—I want to calculate the odds of finding an exact duplicate of a ring where I thought I'd lost it, even though I hadn't really lost it in the first place.

Triple Double Yokes

by Capri Brock

It was going to be our first holiday season since moving to Colorado. We decided that we wanted to host Christmas dinner with the extended family. We invited over a few cousins, their parents and my grandparents. It was going to be a full house, but we were excited to have a family get together.

As children that dislike ham-no matter how much my mother tried to persuade us-we were going to serve a second Thanksgiving dinner; turkey, mashed potatoes and gravy, green bean casserole, cranberry sauce, corn, hard-boiled eggs and a variety of other vegetables. My mother hates deviled' eggs, so we only serve hard-boiled eggs when we host a meal.

It was quite a busy morning getting everything prepared for when the family showed up. My cousin surprised us and came about 1/2 hour early to tell us all that she had a surprise for her mother, my aunt. She showed us a shirt that had been my great-grandmother's that said, "World's Greatest Grandma!" My cousin was going to present the shirt to her to announce that she was expecting. She wanted our help to stage the gifting of the shirt. So we made a plan and all vowed to keep the secret.

The other guests arrived and after a bit of small talk, we all sat down to a big dinner. As per tradition my grandfather led grace. "Dear Lord, Thank you for this holiday and this bountiful food on this table. May this food nourish our bodies, in Jesus name we pray, Amen."

Everyone started to dig in and served up their plates. We discussed what we had received for Christmas that morning. When my cousin started to peel her hard-boiled egg, "Oh, wow! Look at that, there are two yolks in my egg."

"Oh, cool, you know what that means," my mother said off-handedly.

"No, what?" asked my cousin.

"Someone is pregnant!" my aunt interjected before my mom could speak. My aunt was superstitious and believed in signs and omens.

"Oh..." my cousin went quiet and changed the topic quickly.

Dinner and conversation continued, until my mother started peeling her egg. "No, way! Look!" As my mom held up her egg- sure enough, there were two yolks in her egg too.

My aunt came unglued, jumped out of her seat and yelled "SOMEONE HERE IS PREGANT! And I want to know who it is and I want to know now! WHO IS IT?!?" She looked around the table, one by one, staring down every last female in the room.

"Don't you give me that look," my 71-year-old grandmother said with quite a bit of sarcasm in her voice, "You know full-well it isn't me."

My aunt looked at the next female at the table... "Yeah right, you have got to be kidding me! I already had my kids, besides I've been surgically altered," my mom laughed.

Next...

"It would have to be Immaculate Conception, if it was me." I stated, trying to get out of that hot seat as quickly as I could. I was only 15 at the time.

"Ummm, doubt it," said my cousin. My aunt stared longer at her than all the rest, but failing to get the confession she needed, she moved to the next one at the table.

She even stared down my 11-year-old sister, who replied,—a little creeped out, "Ummm why would you look at me?!?!"

Since no one was fessing up to her accusations, she sat back down and started to eat the rest of her dinner. But she kept her eyes on all the ladies at the table trying to figure out who wasn't telling her something. It was a very uneasy rest of the dinner for my cousin as the talk never got off the eggs.

"It could mean prosperity."

"It always means good luck..."

"Not in England."

"It means someone is pregnant," my aunt muttered disappointed.

As we finished dinner and cleaned up, my cousin asked for everyone's attention in the living room and asked her mother to come and sit front and center. My cousin announced there was still one more present to give out before we got to dessert. My aunt did as she was told and sat down; my cousin presented her with a gift.

My aunt started to unwrap the present and pulled out a shirt. Before any one of us could read what it said, she screamed "I KNEW IT! It was you!"

Instead of a great loving surprise moment, my aunt gloated about knowing things psychically. My poor cousin's big announcement ended being anti-climatical thanks to the eggs giving away her secret early.

At this point we decided, it was getting quite ridiculous and we needed to open the rest of the eggs to see if there were any more double yolks, now that the secret was out and all the rest of the ladies in the family were safe from my aunt's interrogations. Sure enough there was one more egg that had a double yolk.

Researchers say that about 1 in 1,000 eggs have double yolks and we had three out of a dozen eggs. The odds of that are close to a billion to one.

The family classified this as the biggest spoiler alert of all time and ever since we have all been wary about opening hard boiled eggs in front of my aunt.

Angel's Protection

"If you knew who walked beside you at all times, you could never experience fear again."

-A Course in Miracles

The Invisible Hand

by Floyd Blake

We lost our son John in 1987 when he was just 31 years old. And ever since that day, he has worked to literally prove how close he still is to us. During the viewing of his body, I asked him for a sign that he was with us. Right then the flowers at the front of the chapel acted like a stiff breeze had just blown them around. From that moment on, whenever I was in church and I heard the song lyric, "In the rustling grass, I hear him pass, He speaks to me everywhere." I remember that moment and know my son is still with me and it gives me comfort.

That is a nice story, and it could be explained away by those who don't want to believe in angels, but the following story... is much harder to dismiss.

My wife and I were driving from Colorado to Idaho to visit our grandchildren. We were driving across I-80 in Wyoming, and as usual, there was a very strong cross wind.

We were driving in a Bronco and dragging a small trailer behind. We always brought along a small trailer to sleep in when we visited. We found that if we didn't need to pay for a hotel, we could stay longer. Our grandchildren were very small still (under 10-years-old) and we loved spending time with them.

Somewhere between Little America and Evanston on I-80, we heard a conversation on the CB radio. "The White Bronco hauling the trailer just lost the license plate on the trailer." My wife and I perked up, and tuned into the conversation.

"Well, he's got an antenna—maybe he can hear this."

"Attention in the Bronco, the license plate on your trailer was just ripped off by the wind."

I pulled over to look to see if it was us—and indeed, our license plate was gone.

I knew roughly what mile marker it must have been at based on the CB conversations. But at best, that would bring us into about a 2 mile potential search area. And in a strong Wyoming wind, who knew how far we'd actually have to search to find it.

The Colorado license plates at that time were kelly green, with metal flake paint in them. It was fall, but there wasn't any snow on the ground, just green grass. So looking for a green license plate in green grass when we weren't quite sure where we lost it was going to take a pretty serious effort.

The nearest exit was almost 5 miles away, so we decided to go there and turn around to get closer to the search area. As we got closer to where we figured it must have been, we saw what we thought was a sign hanging on a fence. It was, of course, on the other side of the highway. But it was a small kelly green rectangle. Not believing that our license plate would just be hanging there waiting for us to find it, we didn't even get hopeful, until we got very close, but as we approached, we could see that it indeed was our license plate.

It appeared to us as if the license plate was just hanging there waiting for us to find it, but there wasn't anything holding it up—except quite possibly, an invisible hand.

We still had another mile or more to go until the next exit. We carefully measured (to the tenth of mile—using the odometer) where we had seen it. We calculated the distance to the exit and drove the same length back down the other side of the Interstate.

We stopped about where we thought it was, yet the license plate wasn't on the fence anymore. But we found it! Our calculations got us within about 20 feet of it when we stopped. It was just a minute or two after stopping and walking around when we found our kelly-green license plate disguised cleverly in the green grass.

We would never have found it if John hadn't held it up there for us to find.

I never doubted from that point on, that my son John traveled with us on those long drives to see his nieces and nephews.

Black Mustang

by EJ Thornton

One night during my sophomore year of high school (circa 1977), I was coming home from a high school dance. One of my best friends, Krystal was riding in the car with me.

The night was dark. There was no moon and even though we lived in what would be called suburbs, there weren't any street lights on the stretch of road we were driving on.

We approached our turn and I was just about ready to make the turn when I heard an incredible scream. So I slammed on the brakes and didn't make the turn.

Just then a black mustang with his headlights turned off sped by doing about 60 mph. If we had taken the turn, we surely would have been hit at high speed and critically injured or worse.

The car speeding by us shocked us of course. But the following conversation shock us both more!

"Wow. Thank you. When did you see the car coming?" I asked Krystal.

"What do you mean?"

"You screamed. I figured you saw the car coming."

"I didn't scream, I didn't see it. I thought you screamed." Krystal said.

"I didn't scream either. I didn't see it either." I shook my head trying to figure it out.

"So who screamed?" Krystal asked.

"I don't know," I answered, "but whoever screamed saved our lives."

"I know," Krsytal quietly agreed.

We'll never know what happened, but we do know what didn't happen. Neither of us were the one who screamed, because neither of us saw the threat coming.

Angels protected us that night from turning in front of a speeding black mustang on a dark, moonless road.

QT Something Something

by John Craig

It was August 10, 2005 and we lived in Nebraska. I was "camping" on the living room floor with Makayla, our 7-year-old granddaughter. My wife Jeanie was sleeping in our bedroom by herself.

Jeanie died that night, suddenly, unexpectedly, and with minimum discomfort of a brain aneurysm.

Based on what I found in the morning, she had finished reading a book for the evening, put the book mark in it and closed it. She got up out of bed, most likely to go to the bathroom, but never made it to the door.

The coroner said she was unconscious before she even fell to the floor. I could tell this was accurate because she hadn't even tried to catch her fall. I found her in the morning, and the grandkids never did see her or experience any direct trauma from the event.

Jeanie had always said she didn't want to lie in a hospital bed for a long time, so she really did die the way she wanted to. I just believe that she went way too early in life at only 54 years of age!

Some people know when they are going to go, and I believe Jeanie must've felt or suspected something as just a couple of days before her death, she made me promise to take care of the grandkids if anything happened to her. Of course I agreed—and I would have taken care of them even if I hadn't promised her that day. I always wondered about that question though—did she know she'd be dead just a few days later?

I need some answers and some closure. I had neither.

For the first few weeks after her death, I kept praying that perhaps she could come to me in my dreams. I also asked her, if at all possible, to help from where she's at with the raising of our two grandkids that we both loved so much.

Jeanie didn't appear in my dreams for weeks, and I was very frustrated and getting depressed about it. Finally, she appeared in two dreams during the same week.

In my first dream, she was in the driver's seat of our car, with me leaning in through the window trying to help her with something. She was trying to call someone on a phone, and she wanted me to help push the buttons to make the call. We had to hurry because she had to drive away, and I also knew I would soon have to wake up. (My dreams of her were lucid in this sense.)

She told me several very important messages too, but the only thing I could remember when I woke up was the phrase "QT something something." The "QT" was very clear, and very important sounding, but the rest was a jumble. I called my daughter the next morning to tell her about my dream and I emphasized that if anything having to do with a phrase starting with "QT" happened, I'd sure pay attention!

In the second dream, Jeanie came up to me with a big smile on her face. She appeared very happy. I asked if it was legal for us to kiss. We did kiss briefly (too quickly) and then she drifted over to do something important again, with us both realizing she should hurry before I had to wake up.

She once again was struggling to dial a telephone. I woke up, feeling both happy and sad at the same time.

The next day I called my son in Colorado and we talked about my two dreams.

He reported also having two dreams involving his mom, and the theme in both of his dreams was "hair." He said in one dream Jeanie handed him a bunch of her own hair she'd apparently cut herself. I worked to figure that out. I wondered if there was some message we were missing. Two dreams of attempted phone calls and two involving her hair. That night it occured to me that there was one person of importance in Jeanie's life that I'd forgotten to call or write to about her passing away; her hair dresser Barb who still lived in Colorado. I called my son the next day, and he immediately drove over to tell Barb the news. She had not heard the news, and she was glad Adam got the message to her.

That message could perhaps have been "coincidence" and/or wishful thinking, hoping that Jeanie was really communicating with us. Even so, it makes sense and I feel that our interpretation was quite plausible.

The QT message, however, is what has me convinced more than ever that she indeed was able to get messages or warnings through. Of course, I don't know what they are, but it sure seems like there are some strict rules and limitations on communications between here and there.

A week or so after those two dreams, when visiting the doctor, I was just so understandably sad. I asked her if perhaps I could take an antidepressant medication to help me through. She suggested a relatively new drug called Lexapro, which for most people had been really successful at treating situational depression. I started on Lexapro on that Wednesday, and by the weekend I was experiencing several side effects, all of which are normal while getting used to the drug.

However, on Sunday, twice I experienced something uncomfortable with my heart. It was kind of like a palpitation, but it seemed like my heart was way out of whack for nearly a full minute each time. All I could do was just stand there holding my breath while waiting for it to get back in sync and feel normal again. Then it happened all over again. I was suddenly very scared!

After the second episode, I decided to get on the Internet to see if there were any other side effects of Lexapro that might not have been listed on the insert.' I came across one, a description of a very rare side effect, sometimes fatal, having to do with the rhythm of the heart. It was often associated with an overdose of Lexapro. That caught my eye, so I read further. The condition is called "QT interval prolongation."

Well, this about floored me, because of the important phrase I recalled Jeanie trying to tell me in my first dream! QT something something... Now I knew what those words were that I couldn't make out!

I quit the Lexapro on the spot, and since then I've felt much better... for a multitude of reasons!

The most interesting part of this was the sequence of the dreams and the events. I had the dream of the warning about QT something something weeks before I ever got on the drug.

How did she know?

I won't likely get the answers while I'm still on this plane of existence, but it makes me wonder about the ability of these Angels to travel back and forth in time.

I've had some more dreams about Jeanie and they are sweet. It is bittersweet to wake up to a world without her. But it is comforting to know that she isn't far away and can still pitch in when it's important.

Angel Ranger

by Cathy Peterson

My close friend Ellen's 10-year-old daughter had been invited to participate in a pageant and her daughter had worked for most of a year to earn enough money to buy the required advertising, which bought her entry into the pageant and pre-paid a hotel room for 3 days.

Ellen's struggle with her husband's alcoholism was hitting an all-time high, probably due to the stress of the impending trip, but the alcoholism problem was years in the making. Ellen came to a breaking point and left her husband at a care facility the day before they were supposed to take the trip from Idaho to California for her daughter to compete.

Desperate to figure out how to still make the trip without her husband, because her daughter had worked tirelessly on her goal, she called me.

"I've got some vacation coming," I said. "Let me see if I can get the time off and the boys and I will come with you."

I knew what I was proposing... a trip with me and my two boys and her and her three kids—all 10-years old and under. It would be an adventure...

I was able to get the time off and we all loaded up the car and headed out to California!

We felt like this had all been arranged, everything happened so smoothly, great weather, clear roads, beautiful scenery, and happy kids! This had happened for a reason and it was a good thing we got Ellen away from all the stress of sending her husband to rehab (an 8-day intensive in-patient program). This way she could keep her promise to her daughter and relax and unwind a bit away from her stressful homelife.

We just felt surrounded and protected by angels the whole trip. It was an amazing feeling.

The pageant went well and after it was done, we took the kids to Disneyland, the ocean and ate at fun restaurants. It was a great vacation.

For the trip back, we planned on driving through Yosemite, a place that I loved and that Ellen and her kids had never seen. But traveling with 5 small kids made getting out of the hotel and on to the road early quite challenging.

We drove and drove and drove. We stopped for a quick bite at Burger King and then drove the windy mountain roads into the Yosemite National Park. For the first time on the trip, we had a harrowing drive, not because of the road conditions, but because two of the kids got car sick thanks to the winding roads combined with fast food. We had to pull over to take care of them. It was getting later and later in the day, but we finally made it into the Park and were able to drive around to see the amazing sites for a little while. Night fell quickly.

After looking at the map, we realized the nearest hotel was still about a 3-hour drive away. The kids were hungry and this day hadn't gone at all by plan. By this time of the night, we had planned to be about 200 miles further down the road.

We pulled over to look at maps more closely to decide

which was the best route to go, when suddenly there was a tap on the window.

It was a park ranger, so I rolled the window down to talk to him. "Can I help you folks?" he asked.

"We're just trying to figure out the best route out of the park. We didn't mean to stay this late and we can't drive another three hours to get the kids to the hotel we planned to get to."

"I see," he said. "Obviously, you won't be able to stay in the Park. People book their reservations about a year in advance, sometimes more. And you can't stay here much longer. We've got to keep the roads clear of cars. But the lodge is right around that next turn. Why don't you pull into that parking lot. They will help you with the nearest out-of-park accomodations. I'm sorry, but you'll probably have to drive quite a while still. They'll help you as much as they can."

We thanked him and he left.

We didn't see where he went or which direction he went. But we didn't question it too much. We knew if we didn't do what he said, he'd be back and not quite as chipper and helpful.

He was right, we'd been sitting along the side of the road, but the lodge was just around the next turn. We felt a little foolish.

I got out of the car and went into the lodge to find out what I could about where we could stay that night. We had no camping gear and sleeping 5 kids in a car sounded pretty miserable, but so did driving 200 more miles. Everyone in the car hoped I would come back with good news, but our prospects seemed pretty bleak.

I went into the lodge and explained our situation. Then I asked, "Can you help us with the nearest out-of-park accomodations?"

"Unless you'd like to stay here..." the desk clerk said.

"The Ranger said that everything in the park is booked solid," I answered.

"We usually are, but this must be your lucky day, because we just got a cancellation. That just doesn't happen around here. People usually book months in advance. We're always sold out!"

"I would very much like the room," I said.

"Cabin okay?" the desk clerk clarified.

"Absolutely!"

I booked the room and ran out of the lodge, waving a key in my hand!

"I booked us a room!"

"How did you do that?" Ellen asked in amazement.

I regaled her the story from inside.

"Wow," she explained. "Thank God for that Ranger or we'd still be on the side of the road!"

"I know... They said that we had to be the luckiest people, because cancellations are so rare here!" She and I looked at each other, not wanting to say what we were thinking in front of the kids, but we both knew that ranger had been sent to help us—specifically.

The kids all cheered and we went to the little cabin we'd rented. We had a restful night and woke up to the splendor of Bridal Veil Falls—a sight wc hadn't even noticed the night before in our panic!

If that ranger hadn't directed us, we'd have had to drive, exhausted on dark unfamiliar, mountain roads with 5 small kids in the car. We're not sure if the ranger was real or a manifested angel—but since "Angel" means messenger in Greek, we decided that no matter what, he had been an angel for us!

Bird-Greensleeves

by John Craig

A few years ago, when my grandson Dakotah was about 8-years-old, his wrist area swelled and the diagnosis was possible cancer, caused by his congenital condition of osteochondroma (bone bumps). We were horrified, yet numb, while waiting for further tests to be undertaken. We had just moved from Colorado to an ancient, very small but cozy house near the south edge of Wahoo, Nebraska. With all the stress of a new job, a new town, the promise of a whole new life for all of us, we sure didn't need this news.

That night while sitting around the dining room table in the small kitchen area, I noticed Dakotah staring intently into the dark of the adjacent living room area.

After a bit I asked him, "What are you looking at, Dakotah?"

His casual and matter of fact answer immediately caught my attention. "Just looking at my friend."

Not sure what to think, I decided to play along with his imagination, being careful not to lead him in any specific direction, but just to see if I could get to the bottom of whatever was going on in his mind. "Who is your friend?" I prompted.

"He's an Indian and he said he's protecting me." Dakotah had never been one to make up stuff like this, and he seemed very sure and nonchalant with his answers, so I kept going, fascinated with where his creative imagination was taking him, while starting to wonder if someone might actually be there to help Dakotah. Considering the magnitude of the news about Dakotah's arm we'd received earlier that day, I found myself hoping for the latter, even while my scientific, skeptical mind knew the explanation was likely just his young imagination. Still, the way Dakotah answered made the hair on my neck stand straight up!

"Okay, what tribe does he belong to?" I asked.

"He's Pawnee," replied Dakotah. I was surprised at how easily his answers kept coming. Dakotah was in the first grade, I didn't know if he'd studied Indian tribes at all by then. I know I hadn't.

"What's his name?" I asked.

Somewhat hoping Dakotah would finally come back with an "I don't know" or something to clinch the explanation. However, after staring into the dark for several long seconds, Dakotah confidently stated, "He says his name is Bird-Greensleeves."

I had to ask one last question, "Where does he live?"

Dakotah replied, "He says he lives in the barn out back, and he's here to help me."

My wife and I looked at each other wide-eyed, wondering about Dakotah's answers.

The following day, on an impulse, I researched the history of Wahoo and its surroundings on the Internet. I came across one of those ancient photos of the town, when there were but a handful of buildings, mostly located between the old railroad tracks and the creek in the distance. Amazingly, the house we were living in was in the photo! Also in the photo was a small barn-like building out back. A little more research revealed that members of the Pawnee Nation had lived in a major encampment in the area, about a block away from our house along the banks of the creek.

Dakotah's tests on his arm a few days later came back negative. No cancer!

Like so many other amazing angel stories, there's no way to prove absolutely that Bird-Greensleeves really did hang around to help Dakotah, but personally, I'm convinced he did. And I'll always be grateful for his great caring, kindness, generosity and protection.

Rockies' Angel

by Amy Collette

My mother is a huge sports fan. She got tickets to go with her co-workers to a Colorado Rockies game, and she invited me to go. I worked in downtown Denver, close to where the Rockies play, so she picked me up from work to go to the afternoon game.

We drove around looking for a place to park, and there weren't many that didn't cost a bundle. She wanted to park in a less expensive lot close to my office. I said that was fine, as long as it was still daylight when we got back to the car " this was a dangerous place to be after dark.

So we parked and walked the few blocks to the game. She had really dressed for the game " full Rockies paraphernalia, including a white and purple cowboy hat! We had a great time cheering on our Rockies.

After the game her friends wanted to grab some dinner. I suggested that we move the car at that point, knowing that we would go out and forget to move the car to a safer location. My mom said no, and sure enough, exactly what I was afraid of happened, we stayed too long and allowed darkness to fall without moving the car.

After dinner and a few beers, it was dark, after 10:00pm. I was really worried about us two women walking in that neighborhood to the car. The men in the party had already left, and Mom thought I was being dramatic and overprotective of her. I wanted her friends to drive us over to our lot, but she said I was being ridiculous, it was only a few blocks.

After a couple of blocks we were away from the party scene of the post-ballgame restaurants and bars " the streets were dark and very quiet. She took my arm and we began walking faster. Across the street a man was walking parallel to us. He looked over at us and nodded. This did not reassure us, so we walked even faster.

Despite our speed, the man crossed the street, which meant he was just behind us. I began to feel really terrified. I thought for sure he was going to mug us. Even though he was a small man and we are not tiny women, he could be armed or otherwise dangerous.

Then he spoke. "Where are you ladies parked?" Even though his words could be taken as aggressive, when I heard his voice I relaxed.

Something about him made me feel safe, so I told him, "We're in the lot in the next block." Mom ribbed me with her elbow, thinking I shouldn't have told him.

He said, "I'll keep an eye on you until you get there. You know this is a bad neighborhood."

I whispered, "Yes, I know. And thank you."

The rest of the block we walked in silence. Mom and I started across the lot, just a short distance to our car. The man stayed on the sidewalk and watched us get into the car. As I got in the car, I turned around to thank him again—but he was gone. I looked in every direction and he was nowhere to be seen.

Mom and I both knew as we drove away that we had just had the protection of a guardian angel.

Tow Truck from Heaven

by Christine Grininger

My mother had been away for several days away on a work-related road trip. The drive back was not just exhausting, it became dangerous.

As the daylight receded, it became very challenging to navigate the slick, snowy roads toward home. Lots of open space occupied the many highway miles between the tiny Ohio communities. In spite of travelling at a snail's pace, her vehicle hit a patch of ice and skidded off the road into a recessed embankment.

Panic overwhelmed her thoughts. She wondered whether or not she'd be seen in the dark ravine. Anxiety consumed her mental state. Attempting to quell her fears, she fervently prayed to be rescued. Cold and frightened, she feared that it was inevitable that her snow blanketed car would be invisible until the morning light.

Time crawled by while she waited for any car to pass. Behind her in the distance she saw a pair of oncoming headlights. The deep snow outside caused her to consider if she could climb up the ditch in time to flag down the vehicle for help. Momma then noticed the approaching truck appeared to be heading off the road in her direction. A gentleman arrived with his wife and child in the front seat of a tow truck. Momma watched with surprise while he jumped out of his truck with complete ease and offered to tow her back to the pavement. Before long he hooked up her disabled vehicle and safely pulled it back to the edge of the road.

Momma thanked him profusely, yet felt embarrassed to reveal that she only had a couple of dollars in her purse. She offered to mail him payment but he told her not to worry since he was glad to be of help. Compelled to acknowledge his kindness, my mother took note of the business name painted on the tow truck door. The Good Samaritan returned to his family and quietly drove away on the snowy highway.

The following day Momma was on a mission to track down the tow truck driver. She searched for his business name in all of the community phone books in the areas she'd travelled but could find no listing for *All Soul's Towing*.

Midnight Visitor

by John Craig

I was "camped out" in a sleeping bag on the floor of my home office in Alaska one night in 1986, when a strange but intense pain in my abdomen suddenly became unbearable. Hardly able to breath, I managed to get myself into the passenger side of our family car so my wife could drive us to the emergency room.

After quickly ruling out all the obvious potential threats, such as a heart attack, we spent a couple hours in the emergency room simply in "wait and see" mode, with the pain slowly subsiding. Finally, I was released with instructions to return the next day for further testing. We drove home, and about 2 or 3 in the morning, I crawled back into my sleeping bag next to my son, who never did wake up through all the events of that night.

Moments later, while in that mental awareness state halfway between awake and asleep, I suddenly had the clear thought to swallow something on the back of my tongue, and I was "told" to just keep my eyes closed and that it would help me. Was I imagining this? Were there aliens in my room? Angels?

The messaging was calming and comforting, so I did keep my eyes closed, and I did feel like I swallowed something tiny. Then I fell asleep peacefully and forgot all about the stressful night.

The next day, I felt fine, but we visited the emergency room to do the testing anyway. I had never felt any pain that intense in my life, where just the act of breathing was becoming difficult, so I wanted answers, and mostly I never wanted that to happen again! They drew blood samples and performed an ultrasound as first diagnostic steps, and then we went home to wait for a call from the lab with all the results.

When the call came, it was not good. The blood tests showed something very major was going on with my liver, and the ultrasound revealed a 4 cm lump on my liver. It was Friday, so they immediately made an appointment for early Monday to do a complete CAT scan and other tests. We had plans to fly to Seattle for the weekend, and since there was nothing else to do until Monday, we went ahead and enjoyed that quick weekend getaway as best we could. I clearly recall looking at my kids and my wife that weekend in the pool at the motel, wondering how many more enjoyable moments like those I might have left.

The Monday testing went smoothly, and once again we went home to wait for the call from the Doctor. When it came, he sounded very puzzled, and asked that I come in to the office for yet another consultation and perhaps other tests.

I felt fine, but the Doctor kept looking at me with the most interesting, quizzical looks. He asked a bunch of questions, such as if I'd eaten any polar bear liver, or raw seafood recently. His openness and honesty caught me off guard, as he explained that he was completely mystified with my case. The CAT scan showed only scar tissue at the site on my liver where the 4 cm lump had been just three days before, and a second round of blood tests showed my liver function was nearly back to normal.

That was, of course, the good news. The concern was we had no idea what, if any, the bad news might be.

I knew he was really mystified, and perhaps concerned, when he took me with him back to his personal office where we both started thumbing through his medical books, looking for some sort of possible explanation. He had other patients waiting in the lobby, so this royal and special treatment had me feeling good and respected, but also apprehensive about what the Doctor was thinking. Finally, he concluded I should just go on with my life, and report back immediately if anything else happened. There was nothing else to be done, and sometimes there simply are no explanations. I could live with that, so that's exactly what I did, and I've never had a repeat episode since.

So what really happened to me that night? How and why did I have what appeared to be a near complete liver-failure and tumor situation completely reverse itself over a single weekend? At the time, I didn't take too seriously the "swallow this" message later that night, but looking back on it, with the results of all the testing a few days later, I believe some angelic or other-worldly intervention is a very likely possibility. I don't question its reality or purpose, and I'm very grateful for my life ever since.

Another Type of First-Responder

by Cathy Peterson

I was 17-years-old and I lived in Fresno with my two siblings and my mother. My mother also let her boyfriend's friends stay with us frequently. This day we had a few people staying in the house and a couple of them were working on a car in the garage.

It was early afternoon, I was in the living room playing on my guitar, lost in my own world. I was the only one in the house awake. One of the fix-it guys was asleep upstairs. Everyone else was out shopping or at school.

Suddenly I smelled smoke. I could tell it was coming from the garage. I put down my guitar and ran to the kitchen and up to the door to the garage. I was just about to fling it open when I was stopped in my tracks by a not-so-small voice that told me not to open the door. It was such a powerful and strange message that I paid attention to it even in my rush to find out the source of the smoke. I knew I could see inside the garage if I went out front, so I did that.

Sure enough, it was on fire and the cars inside were already engulfed in flames.

I ran inside to wake the houseguest and then ran to the neighbor's to call the fire department. I was able to go back in the house and rescue a few things, like my guitar, our pets and a couple valuables.

When the fire-fighters arrived, the elementary school was letting out and the kids were running all around in the street in front of the house to get a better view. Their angels had to have been working overtime too, because miraculously with all the chaos of the fire and fire engines the tragedy didn't get any worse.

One of the fire-fighters asked me to tell him what had happened.

"I smelled smoke and I was about to open the garage door attached to the kitchen, but something stopped me, a voice or something. I don't know, suddenly I got scared and ran outside to look inside the garage."

"Well that voice saved your life, young lady," he said. "If you had opened that door you would have been engulfed in flames and likely killed instantly."

I didn't say much, I was stunned by what he said. I was stunned by the fact that my house and most of our belongings were gone and we had to suddenly rebuild our lives. I was the oldest, so I took care of my mom and my family as best I could as we moved on to the next phase of our lives.

But I never forgot what that firefighter told me and I have wondered ever since who or what really stopped me from opening that door that day. I think I know...

Physical Proof

*Do not neglect to show hospitality
to strangers, for thereby,
some have entertained angels unawares.*

-Hebrews 13:2 RSV

Proof

by EJ Thornton

John always loved a challenge. He was a graduate student and associate professor of physics at a Colorado University, when he died in a climbing accident. John was also incredibly playful and loved his family, his wife and son, brothers and sisters, parents, cousins, etc. John knew the importance of family.

About five years after his death, our lives had gotten back to normal, until barely after the first of the year, my 89-year-old grandmother (father's mother) had a mild bout with cancer. Luckily, it was found at a very early stage, and was completely treatable. Then about one month later, she slipped on ice trying to get into her front door and fell onto a concrete stoop. A fall that might have broken anyone else's hip or worse, only broke her pinky finger. Her sweater caught the door and greatly lessened the impact of her fall. We all knew that an angel was watching over her for both of these events. And both of these events took place during the planning of a big 90th birthday bash in her honor.

Many family members lived in other states, and the last time they were all together was at John's funeral. However, all of the out-of-town grandkids decided to bring the great-grandkids and celebrate with her. Later, they told all shared with one another that they hadn't planned on coming, due to finances or work, but because of Grandma's recent troubles, they all made the extra effort to celebrate this milestone birthday with her. After all, everybody would rather come to a birthday party, than a funeral.

My brothers, sisters and all the kids stayed with my folks. We could feel that John was there too. We talked about him quite a bit. But my father didn't mention anything about a very vivid dream that a distant family member had shared with him—about John.

My sister-in-law was sure that John—since he was such a trickster—was making things break in her hand. Everytime it happened, (and it happened several times that weekend—and only to her), she joked, "John, quit picking on me!"

The mood was incredibly festive and we knew, if John could be with us, he would have been. We all found peace in that thought.

The morning of the party, there was a surprise snow storm, heavy and thick; perfect snowball-fighting snow. The out-of-town relatives didn't pack for winter. It was spring where they were from. So Mother dug out a big bag, full of scarves, gloves and mittens. People put on whatever they could grab and went out to play.

Left inside, however, was my two year old son—who was named in part to honor John. The adults and the big kids were playing too rough for him. So he found something else to do. No one was quite sure where he went, but when he came back down the hall, he was sporting John's little league baseball cap.

My father gasped! No one knew why Dad had such a dramatic response to this, until he told us about the dream.

"It was predicted," Dad started, "that John would make his presence known and he has. But it was also predicted that someone would find one of his hats. That would be proof-positive he was here and able to connect with us."

Everyone who knew John, knew it was his handiwork. It was just like him, to rise to the challenge and give us physical evidence of his presence with us.

Well, as a family, we discussed it and yes, we decided it was proof. John had predicted the event. He made it known beforehand in a dream, so that it would be recognized when it happened!

John had delivered his message only to one person, so, it's not like any of the rest of us were looking for a hat of his.

John gave the present, he gave it to the only one in the house who couldn't answer questions about it, a two year old boy. A boy who had been named to honor him and actually had the exact same initials as were inscribed in the hat: J. Blake.

So perfectly like John, this event proved his personality and playfulness were still quite present. His proximity to the family was undeniable.

The people of this family are spiritual and don't delight in ghost stories, but they do feel the love of God and their departed loved ones. Even though John is gone from this plane of existence, he is still alive and well and loving us every second. It just goes to show, Heaven isn't really that far away.

Proof—Part 2

by EJ Thornton

One night about five years later, my son (J. Blake) and I were on our way home. We were driving on the highway late at night. Suddenly the car just lost all power, it was still rolling, but it went from 70 MPH to about 10 MPH instantly.

Of course, I looked in all the mirrors and all around and was so grateful that I didn't see any cars around me anywhere. Feeling an overwhelming sense of being taken care of, I just gave thanks that we were able to drive to the right-hand shoulder of the highway and crept safely most of the way down an off-ramp.

We called a tow truck and decided that the transmission in my car had just had a catastrophic failure. That car was done for, but gratefully no person was any worse-for-wear. I thanked my brother John for protecting me, because I had an instant sense that he was there. I'm sure that my son and I have our own guardian angels, that were working overtime that night, but I could almost hear John say, "Don't worry, I've got you." I can't explain it, it was just my experience. I was never scared, or upset about the incident. It was almost peaceful.

Proof—Part 3

by EJ Thornton

A few weeks after that, one my authors, Jude took me with her to an event. I don't even remember what kind of event, maybe a concert. There was an "Angel Reader" there and I thought that was interesting, but I didn't engage her. Even though I wrote "*Angel On Board*," I typically stayed away from other "Angel things" because I didn't want someone else's story to bleed into mine. Ironic that now, I'm writing a book like this... But that was why I didn't hire her for a reading.'

A few minutes later however, Jude came up to me with a ticket and announced, "I bought you a present. I bought you an angel reading!"

I put my issues aside and went to meet this woman and let her read my angels.

"I sense a strong male presence," she said.

Don't they all? I thought at that moment, letting my inner-skeptic come out.

"Have you had any major car problems lately?" she asked again. I nodded. "He just wants you to know he was there for you."

I became a believer pretty quick.

"He's showing me your son," she said.

That got my attention.

"He says your son has seen him."

"I don't think so..." I responded, not remembering my life very well apparently. "My son has never said anything about that to me."

"He's pretty insistent that your son has seen him and that you know of the event he's referring to."

Then it dawned on me... "The hat! Oh my, he means when he gave my son the hat."

"He wants you to know he loves you."

"I love you too..." I whispered reasonably choked up.

And that was the end of my angel reading. I went in hesitant and skeptic, but emerged a complete believer, at least in this woman's talents.

Asking for Signs

Trust in the Lord with all thine heart; and lean not unto thine own understanding. In all thy ways acknowledge him, and he shall direct thy paths.

Proverbs 3:5-6
King James Version (KJV)

Pennies from Heaven

by EJ Thornton

I was reading my e-mail on a typical day when I received an Internet order that changed my life. The order form asks the buyer to tell me how they heard of the book they are ordering (in this case *Angel On Board*), because that tells me which portion of my marketing efforts are being effective. Usually, I get a word or two like Friend' or Google' or something terse like that.

On this order, a woman wrote me a desperate letter in that little space, pleading with me to e-mail her more of the book because she NEEDED it. She wanted me to send the book in overnight mail and she'd pay anything it took to have that happen. She proceeded to tell me why she was so anxious to read the rest of the book.

I don't remember this woman's name, but I do remember her angel's name: Tara.

Tara had been killed 18 months prior to the date of this e-mail and her mother was suffering mass denial. In fact, as she was telling me the story of Tara's accident, she told me of her deep denial and admitted that I was the first person she had been able to say this to.

To have someone tell you something that important was so humbling. I was so honored. I was so shook at the significance of this event. I cried for four hours straight.

When I got myself back together, I e-mailed her the chapters and fed-exed her the book and wrote her an e-mail asking her to tell me more about Tara.

She told me about her beautiful daughter and how hard the reality of her leaving had been on her, but when she accidentally' stumbled across my book on the web earlier that day, she'd felt Tara had guided her to it. She started to read the first few chapters that I post online and when the angels spoke in the book, she felt like Tara was telling her the same things. She read until there was no more left to read, cried and cried but finally felt amazing relief.

She told me that everyday since Tara's death, she would find a shiny penny somewhere. She said that she might be cleaning a counter, and just have wiped it clean, then she'd turn away for just a moment and when she turned back, there was a penny. She knew it was a gift from Tara.

When this happened, I was at a crossroads in my life too. I had to choose whether to follow my dream of promoting *Angel On Board* and learning the publishing business so I could do it more effectively or going back into the safety of a job and a career programming computers (which I had done for 20+ years). I had a family to support, but *Angel On Board* as a dream constantly called to me and was very important to me.

One day, when I had to make the decision to quit that high paying computer programming career and take a lesser paying job with a publisher, I asked for a sign.

I turned around, and there on my freshly swept kitchen floor was a shiny new penny. Tara was on my side. I knew this was what I had to do. So, I followed my dream and now here I am, I've owned my own publishing company for 14 years.

Thanks, Tara and thank you, Tara's mom for sharing her with me!

The Agreement

by Christine Grininger

My mother and I enjoyed a delightfully close relationship. During one of our lively discussions we agreed that whenever one of us died we would communicate from the other side. Because of this pact, I felt especially let down when more than 6 months passed after Momma died and still no sign of communication. I was relating my disappointment about this promise to a mutual friend of ours. She then proceeded to tell me that when she was in graduate school she had an assignment in which Momma had participated. It turned out our friend had 4 hours of a tape recorded interview detailing my mother's life story. Through the comfort of hearing her voice again, I received a wonderous message of love.

My next message came a couple of years later. I had decided to reframe a selection of counted cross stitch angels that Momma had sewed for me while she was alive.

In the process of disassembling one of the pictures I discovered a folded note between the cardboard backing and the artwork. Tears filled my eyes when I read the following affirmation: "This is a reminder your Guardian Angel will always be with you to guard and protect you-I love you so much-Momma."

A third message came through one night when I was feeling terribly distressed about a falling out I had with my brother. I had a weepy solo conversation with my Mom telling her how regretful I was that her children weren't getting along.

Eventually, I let it go and comforted myself by picking up a book and reading in bed. I had an urge to glance over at the dresser in my bedroom. What I saw before me captured my attention. A narrow shaft of sunlight spotlighted a framed photo of my Momma. I couldn't have received a better sign of reassurance.

On a Mission from God

by EJ Thornton

I've always believed in the healing power of *Angel On Board*. From the very first reader, I was told of the wonderous and healing stories of those who read it. I knew I had something very, very special on my hands and that this book needed to be released to the world. It did make the world a better place and those who read it felt better after doing so.

My husband at the time was basically the bad guy' of the story, or more precisely the alcoholism he suffered from was, and even though I know he never read the story, he was proud of me for writing the book and he told everyone about it. Ironically, he was one of my best sales people.

He worked at a grocery store in the bakery department and one day Laura, a young woman from the butcher-block came over and asked him about the book. He ended up selling her a copy. She took it home and read it in just a couple of days. She said she loved every bit of it.

Tragically within less than a week, the woman was boating with her husband and there was a terrible accident and Laura's husband was killed. It was awful and we all were so worried about Laura and how she would cope with the tragedy.

Then I worried to myself, what if the stories in *Angel On Board*, upset her? I spun an amazing set of weird scenarios in my head where she might end up being scared when she was alone if she imagined her husband might be with her. I wondered if the images from the book, being so fresh in her head just might do more harm than good right for her at this painful time in her life. I worked myself into such a state, I thought that I should not move forward with my dream of writing until I knew that she was okay and that the book didn't do any damage.

I didn't tell anyone my concerns and I didn't know Laura personally, even though she worked with my husband. So, there wasn't going to be any way that I could ever even casually ask her how she was doing to gauge my concerns. I was almost ready to quit I was so worried.

I gave up on ever being able to put my fears to rest. I started to dismantle my dream of my book. I couldn't move forward with confidence anymore and I had no way to solve my problem.

Until one fateful day that I went shopping in the grocery store where my husband worked. One of his co-workers that I did know very well came running over to me and just about tackled me.

"Did you hear about Laura?" she asked.

"I did," I answered, "it is just awful."

"Yes, it is." She agreed, "but do you want to know what she told me the first time I saw her?"

I nodded.

"She was in total shock when she came home alone for the first time—understandably, but she said she saw your book and picked it up and started to read it again. She said it gave her a lot of comfort. She's so glad she read it just a couple of days before this happened. Things happen for a reason."

"Yes... they do." I stood there, reasonably speechless and totally relieved.

It never ceases to amaze me how the Angels know exactly what you need to hear and find a way to get you to hear it.

I put my full energies back into *Angel On Board* that day and since then it has touched thousands and thousands of readers. I'm so touched by the letters I get and the love I feel from my readers. I'm just so glad I can relax in the fact that it does truly help people, especially those who are hurting. I guess it is on a Mission from God!

Miracle Cure

by Capri Brock

When I was a child, I would get bloody noses with the change of seasons. It is a pretty common condition and not one that too many people raise a fuss about. I was used to it, it had been happening since I was about 4. Now I was 10 and this spring, the bloody noses were worse than they had ever been—in fact, I had several a day and it was starting to get concerning.

It was also embarassing to have so many bloody noses, especially in school and around guests. And we were just about to be deluged with guests. My uncle was getting married and the whole side of my step-dad's family was going to be coming into town.

All I could do was grin and bear it, because the nose bleeds weren't lightening up and we couldn't control them.

On about the third day of my grandma's visit, she, my aunt, my mom and I were driving in the car and I got another bloody nose. My mom was driving, so my aunt and grandma had to scramble to get me enough kleenex to keep from making the mess too big.

"Has this been going on long?" my grandma asked my mom.

"About two weeks," she replied, "but this is worse than it has ever been."

"What can you do about it?" Grandma asked in earnest.

"Not much, hope the weather changes and it settles out," my mom said reasonably defeated about her power to control the situation.

"Well I can do something about it. Pull the car over!"

So, my mother pulled into the nearest gas station and parked the car.

My grandma instructed my aunt and my mother to lay hands on me' and she proceeded to pray, loud, hard and strong. She called in the power of the Holy Ghost, Christ and the Angels. She prayed until my nose stopped bleeding. It really didn't take all that long.

"Wow, thank you," I said to my grandma.

"Don't thank me... Thank the Lord," she instructed me.

So I did that too.

That was the last bloody nose I ever had. I can't explain it, but I'm extraordinarily grateful for it.

Out of Body

by Connie Blake

It was roughly a week after I had major surgery and I was back at my home in suburban Colorado surrounded by my husband and three youngest children. I was starting to have very severe pain in my chest. Not wanting to be someone who worried everyone else and since I was pretty tired of being treated like I was still sick, I hid the fact that I was hurting, excused myself and went to bed.

The pain just got worse and worse and I didn't know what to do. My husband had come to bed as well, and he was sleeping soundly next to me, I didn't want to wake him. So, I decided to get up for a little while to see if sitting up would help, because laying down had not. So, I sat up... or so I thought, because I turned around and still saw my body laying on the bed. Startled, by the sight, I decided to lay back down because I didn't want to be disconnected from my body. But now I was really frightened. My heart started to race and the pain intensified.

I literally was deciding if I could take the pain or if I was going to let it take me, but then I remembered my beautiful family and I knew I had to fight whatever this was. So I prayed.

Then there was a voice, somehow booming, yet gentle and loving, it came from all around me. It was a man's voice and it said, "Roll over Connie or you'll die."

Not wanting to die and figuring the omnipotent voice just might know what was going on, I rolled over and I felt relief.

Still very frightened over both seeing my body on the bed and hearing the voice, I decided to wake my husband and have him take me to the hospital. I was able to touch him right away, thankfully, my hand didn't also leave my body. I didn't really know what to expect at that moment.

He got up and drove me to the ER. My surgeon rushed to meet us. I had survived a blood clot to my lungs. Immediately they put me on Heprin and re-admitted me to the hospital for a few days to monitor me.

My surgeon was astounded. "Honestly, Connie, I don't know how you survived the night. A blood clot to the lungs is almost always fatal. It is a miracle you're still here."

I agreed. I didn't tell him what I experienced for I didn't want him to commit me to another type of hospital, but all the same I was grateful for whoever was looking over me for I know they truly saved my life.

I went home a few days later, fully recovered and renewed spiritually as well. I know either God or one of his angels told me what to do that night. I was and am still very blessed.

Life on Both Sides

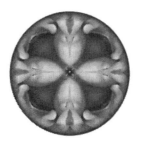

by Sue Scudder

an excerpt from The Voice Across the Veil

Mother's Day, May 1988, four months after giving birth to my daughter, I was wheeled down a hospital hall for emergency surgery to treat a ruptured appendix.

I had never experienced general anesthesia before and felt a premonition that this was not going to be a routine operation. The nurse peered down over my head, a mask covering her nose and mouth. The upside-down view of her long, overdone eyelashes and the thick black eyeliner surrounding each eye was etched in my mind.

"You seem nervous," she said. "Are you worried?"

I nodded.

"This is a common procedure," she attempted to comfort me. "Everything will be fine."

That was all I remembered until sometime later I heard, "Code Blue! Code Blue!" over the intercom and saw two male hospital aides run out of the operating room doors at top speed. My husband and sister-in-law looked at each other in shock—"

I was in that operating room.

At first I didn't realize I was floating above my body. I thought I was dreaming as I witnessed the reactions to this emergency—" my emergency—" from the ceiling of the waiting room.

I was floating in a peaceful, serene, radiant light and felt quite natural. Then in the velvety-smooth brilliance, I floated beyond this world. It was a *familiar* feeling—" like something you know you have experienced but can't quite place.

I found myself in a majestic realm, standing in front of a shining, ornate gate. When it opened, I walked into golden-white light. In the illuminated space, I came upon two large sandstone-colored doors with pillars on either side...and felt very safe, cared for and loved. I entered and peered around a large expansive column. "Where am I?" I thought, walking alone through a building reminiscent of a library. Everything appeared to be made of light-colored marble and I noticed that there were no shadows.

I walked through a maze of enormous white rooms, discovering a large marble bench and pulpit. I looked up. Seven divine spirits of light, immersed in incandescent splendor, looked down upon me and smiled warmly. Their complete and total love embraced me. Noticing I was overwhelmed, they laughed tenderly and asked me to sit on the bench across from them. In the immensity of the room, I felt like a child. I later realized that they were part of the Council of Twelve.

The seven divine spirits of light described to me my life destiny and the path I had chosen for myself long ago. I found myself recalling the plan...and I now *knew* it had to do with my music.

"You will have spiritual guidance and help," they said.

"Yes!" I answered enthusiastically. "And I can do it if I will have your help."

"You won't remember much of this conversation," they said, "until it is time to fulfill your destiny."

I never forgot that meeting, or the very meaningful conversation with those ethereal beings, although the depth of the content did escape me.

"She's waking up!" I clearly heard. I knew I was in the recovery room, even though I wasn't completely back from my trip.

A nurse said, "Susan, I don't want you to be alarmed, but you are completely paralyzed."

"*What*!"

That woke me up! I tried to move. I couldn't even open my eyes. The nurse explained that I had an allergic reaction to the anesthesia, and it would wear off in about ten hours. I was on a respirator—" the only way I could breathe.

I was terrified! I was so aware of everything around me, yet couldn't move a muscle. My senses were exceptionally clear, even though I was trapped in a physical body. Was this what people experience in a coma? I wondered. Helpless entrapment?

Although I couldn't speak or move, I heard every word spoken around me by the caregivers and my loved ones who visited. I may have looked oblivious, but I was present.

Later, another nurse said, "Let's see if she can breathe on her own yet." Terror struck me because I was completely helpless. I had no way of conveying to them that the respirator was still doing the actual breathing for me.

In my mind I screamed, "*No! Don't turn it off. I still need it!*"

The machine stopped and I stopped breathing. They turned it back on immediately. I tried to sleep, to be unconscious and out of my frozen form. I came in and out for a while. After several hours, I could move my eyelids and then communicate by blinking my eyes in answer to questions. Then I could wiggle my toes. It was another five hours before I began to regain control of my physical body. I didn't go home for another three weeks and dearly missed my beautiful new baby, Heather, and my endearing husband, Stephen. Later, I told him about my "dream" of hearing the code-blue warning and seeing the aides running out of the operating room.

Stephen looked startled.

"How did you know that was happening?"

"I was floating just above you. I saw everything that happened!"

After my memorable out-of-body adventure I had a new appreciation for life...and a new understanding: we as humans and the spirit world are very closely connected. I had gone from a physical being to a spiritual being, and back again, in twenty-four hours, coming out more integrated on *both* sides of life. I was the same person. Here *and* there, I was still *me*. Who I was never changed in either form.

Windshield Wipers

by EJ Thornton

I had written *Angel On Board* several years prior and my kids and I were getting used to blaming every interesting event in our life on angels and deriving meaning from them. It was fun knowing that each of my kids—in their heart—knew they were protected. My kids were fearless—still are. They know what's what.

We all started to notice that our car, 1999 Dodge Caravan had an interesting feature. Every now and again, without touching any buttons, the windshield wipers would take one swipe up and down the windshield. It was startling, and it happened reasonably frequently.

We also started to notice that it happened when we were talking about our dreams or something serious. So we decided to blame it on my brother John. Everytime the wipers went off, we decided it was John agreeing with whoever spoke last.

We decided after a few weeks that we'd let him have the last say. He decided arguments and made choices for us. It was good to have him weigh in so often in our lives and feel him so nearby!

Bouncing Books

by John Craig

It had been several years since my wife Jeanie's death and I had gotten used to the one-way conversations I frequently had with her when I needed to sort something out. But those one-way conversations were getting a bit frustrating too. I could almost hear her talk to me. Mostly I heard her words through other people's mouths. I could recognize Jeanie's words, but someone else had to say them so I could hear them.

One day, I went to a bookstore to research what other people had found out about contact with the other side.' I started thumbing through books. I finally just asked, "What do I need to do?"

Just as I consciously asked that question, I saw movement out of the corner of my eye and heard a thump to my left. So I turned quickly. There was nothing there. I went to investigate. I strongly suspected that a book had fallen off a shelf, but there was nothing on the floor and nobody else anywhere near. I had just looked over that bookshelf minutes before and there had been nothing out of place, but now there was. A book had fallen off an upper shelf, bounced and landed back on a lower shelf. It looked for all the world like someone had deliberately placed it there neatly. It just landed with its back out instead of its cover.

The bookcase was against a wall, so this didn't happen because it was hit from the other side. I tried to shake the bookcase, but it was very solid. I couldn't find a reasonable explanation for what I just experienced. Then I remembered the question I had just asked the Universe. "What do I need to do with communicate to the other side?"

I picked up the book that bounced back on the shelf and turned it over to see if there was a clue to my answer. The book was by Jerry and Esther Hicks and it was called, "Ask and It is Given."

I wasn't familiar with the book or its contents, so I read the foreword. The book is written by a couple who channel a spiritual being they've named Abraham. Abraham speaks through Esther and is attempting to enlighten the world.

I received my answer—with a little extra emphasis just in case I wasn't paying attention. "Ask and it is Given."

Tesla

by John Craig

Have you ever felt like you were a pawn in a cosmic dance of events, helping to achieve some goal that only later did you become aware of? This happened to me in 1988, when a whole bunch of seemingly unrelated events unfolded, with me right in the middle, in such a way that it had to be the angels working through me for a specific, very positive result. I'm actually rather honored to have played a part in it all, and they can use me like that any time!

A little back-story will bring the events up to speed. In the early 1980s, I worked with a small group of engineers in the Denver area to create several of the world's largest solar energy fields. We were, and still are, a close group, and even after nearly 30 years since the company disbanded, we still get together each Christmas for a "company party". Our manager, Floyd Blake, was an amazing man, and all of us over the years have commented on how that job was by far the best any of us ever experienced.

In 1987, a year after the funding for the solar company was pulled out from under us all, I found myself working in Alaska.

That's when we received the terrible news that Floyd's son, John, had fallen while rock climbing in Colorado, and had died.

Also in 1987, a very special book was published, titled "Proceedings of the 1986 International Tesla Symposium". This book was published in a very limited edition, with each copy numbered and stamped for authentication, and generally available only to symposium members or authors of the papers in the book. Just as this book was going to press, news of John Blake's untimely death reached the editors. They put a special dedication page in the book, right before John's very interesting and very technical article titled, "The Particle Photon" that is of interest to physics professionals at the leading edge of the field.

A year later, in 1988, I found myself working in Bozeman, Montana with a small group of engineers on optics software under a government research contract. That summer, my favorite boss from years past, Floyd Blake, called to say he and his wife Connie were driving through from Denver to Idaho to visit their other kids, and could they park their camper in our driveway overnight and have a visit? We were delighted at this news, and looked forward to their coming visit at the end of the week.

While at work the next morning, I found myself chatting with one of my co-workers, Kyle, standing just inside the doorway to his office, leaning against his tall bookshelf. Somehow, the conversation came around to the subject of Nikola Tesla and his amazing electrical inventions. I mentioned that I knew someone who had been very interested in Tesla research until his untimely death, and Kyle's eyes got big when I mentioned John's name. He had me turn around to pull a hefty book that I'd been leaning against off his shelf. There in the middle was an article authored by Kyle, and immediately following that one was the dedication page and article written by

John Blake. They had both authored articles for the same Tesla symposium.

I then told Kyle that John's father Floyd was, by an amazing coincidence, going to be in town the very next day. Kyle asked again when John had died, then put two-and-two together to realize that since the book had only recently been published, and only in a very limited edition, there was likely no way that Floyd had received a copy of the book John was published in. We discussed this situation for just a few seconds, when Kyle suddenly made the decision to present his only copy to Floyd. This kindness floored me, but we made plans to all meet for supper the next evening when Floyd and Connie were to be in town, with the plan to present the book to them at that time.

Needless to say, a lot of tears flowed the next evening when Kyle presented the book to Floyd and Connie. They had heard of the book that John was published in, but repeated calls to various people in the past had not resulted in any possible way for the Blakes to get a copy. All the numbered copies were gone, and there were no plans to ever publish it again. They had given up on ever seeing John's article. But there it was, stamped copy number 64 of the rare and valuable book being presented to them by a kind stranger in the middle of Montana.

Looking back on the events leading up to getting that copy of the book into Floyd and Connie's hands, a lot of "what if's", and "how amazing is that coincidence" kept popping up. I'm absolutely convinced John, or other helper angels, worked through me and Kyle, and probably other people as well, to miraculously get that important book into the hands of his parents under seemingly impossible circumstances. I'm thrilled to have played a part in the steps involved.

Doorbells

by John Craig

A few weeks after my wife passed away, I was riding home in my car, once again having one of those frustrating one-way conversations with Jeanie, wishing with all my might that we could once again just have a simple chat, a talk about the days events, just the enjoyable little talk that we all take for granted until those conversations are no longer possible. I ended my diatribe with a request, "Jeanie, if there's any way, can you give me a sign that you're okay?" After a little thought I clarified my request, "A bell, any bell, just let me hear a bell out of the blue or something and I'll know it's you. Can you do that?"

I arrived home and went about the evening, making supper for my two grandkids, checking my email, and going on with life in general. Suddenly, the doorbell rang, although it sounded weak and some how distant and different. I went to the front door and nobody was there. Immediately I recalled my request to hear a bell, so I stood there for a couple minutes trying to skeptically determine why in the world that front doorbell would have rung, and why had it sounded so funny?

Suddenly I was jolted out my reverie by the same sound once again. The doorbell rang for the second time, once again sounding flat and distant. I was still standing near the front door, so I bolted toward it to see if I could perhaps catch some kids playing games with me, or something. Again, nobody was there, and this time I knew that nobody had pushed that button. They would not have had time to exit the front porch, there was no place to hide, and besides all that we could normally hear people walking on our front porch from inside the house. I was puzzled.

For the third time the doorbell rang, this time while I was standing right there at the front door. Still nobody there, of course. I wanted to believe it was Jeanie, but my skeptical, scientific mind wanted a clear answer. The sound of that doorbell was real, and the laws of physics demanded an explanation!

I got a ladder, took the cover off the doorbell ringer near the ceiling in the dining room, and removed the batteries. A quick trip downstairs to my computer area where I had a battery tester revealed what I half expected, the batteries were dying. It had never happened to us in the several years we lived in that house, but when the batteries got weak, the doorbell was designed to weakly signal the fact, repeatedly, until you either replaced them or they ran out completely.

So, was this an answer by Jeanie to my request that she provide the sound of a bell? I like to think so. What are the odds that those batteries would just happen to run low within an hour of my request? Also, this event was part of a repeating pattern, where the odds of any one of the events was plausible, but when they keep happening over and over again, well, the laws of probability demand some further explanation! When I take into account several other important and amazing communication events, one where Jeanie actually saved my life, I simply have to believe this was more than a coincidental event.

Padre Pio

by Othniel J. Seiden

During my research for the book, *The Capuchin—the Life of Padre Pio*, I learned several mysterious and wonderful things about this soon-to-be-saint.

Padre Pio had a well-documented case of the Stigmata or the wounds of Jesus. If you do a web search on Padre Pio, undoubtedly his wounds will show up in the pictures.

I was fascinated by his life and as a medical doctor, I was totally blown-away by the claims of a body temperature of 125 degrees, etc. The truth was harder to write in my historic novel, than the characters that surrounded my novel's hero. The stories that surrounded this man were—at best— unbelievable, yet they had been meticulously documented by doctors and others in the scientific communities.

One of the claims was that his wounds, albeit ugly, bloody and ever-present actually smelled of roses and lilac. I also found this fascinating because there is no logical, scientific or any other reasonable reason that open wounds would smell of flowers. Yet, again, that was documented.

One autumn night as I was walking with my late wife down in our neighborhood and discussing the book I was writing, we pondered if indeed the now-deceased Padre Pio would approve. As if on queue, a gentle breeze blew past us and the scent of roses and lilacs swirled around us for several seconds.

We took it as a good sign...

Singing Baby

by John Craig

My first wife, Jeanie passed away suddenly in 2005, and I've missed her dearly ever since. I've remarried, to a friend Jeanie and I both knew from my previous years working in solar energy. EJ is wonderful person, and I love her dearly too. She lost her brother to a climbing accident, so she has been very understanding and supportive of the occasional grief episodes that pop up out of the blue, for the both of us.

I'm sure I'll always occassionally shed tears for Jeanie for the rest of my life, but it's okay, as I've learned to accommodate those feelings, and to balance them with the wonderful new memories EJ and I are forming as we go on with life.

A few summers ago, EJ and I drove to Yellowstone and Tetons National Parks for our summer vacation. We had a great time, but the sites did bring back a lot of bittersweet memories, as Jeanie had loved that area of the country a lot. Jeanie and I had last visited the area less than a month before she passed away so unexpectedly.

EJ and I took the boat ride across Jenny Lake and hiked the distant trail into the foothills of the Tetons, just as Jeanie and I had done many years before. I pointed out to EJ that Jeanie and I had named our first born daughter Jennifer, because we had visited Jenny Lake while she was pregnant, and Jeanie loved that lake!

It was a beautiful sunny day, with no breeze, and only the sounds of water rushing over the rocks as water from the melting snows high in the Tetons tumbled through the lush forest on the way down hill to Jenny Lake. I was enjoying the hike immensely, pondering the majesty of nature and the universe at its finest.

I suddenly missed Jeanie to the point of near tears, but I halted those feelings and replaced them with a smile of remembrance of how much she had smiled along that very trail, in years gone by. In my mind, I quietly asked for a sign, just a little unique sign, that she was nearby. I even got more specific and asked that somehow, in this quiet deep forest, I might hear some music, just a little music of some sort, and that this improbable event would be a clear signal.

We hiked on, enjoying all the sites and sounds of the Teton forest with its waterfalls and unspoiled natural beauty.

I had pretty much forgotten about my request to hear music somehow, and was thoroughly enjoying sharing the views with EJ. We passed a few other hikers along the trail as they came down the slopes headed back towards the boat dock for the ride back to civilization across the lake. A young couple approached, the father carrying an infant girl in a backpack carrier on his back. The little girl was singing, something very melodic and beautiful sounding. We smiled, and the mother stated in amazement as she passed us, almost apologetic, "She never sings, this is really the first time she's ever sang anything!"

We all listened for a minute to the beautiful melody, deciding that little girl must really like hiking in the Tetons! We then learned that the young family was from Omaha, just a few miles away from where Jeanie and I had lived. What a small world! We parted ways and continued our hike.

Then it all hit me, and I burst into tears of joy. The music, the little girl from Nebraska, the joy of the sightseeing. It was a message to me once again, with way too much symbolism to be mere coincidence. Jeanie was right there—with us!

Marshal, Marshal, Marshal

by EJ Thornton

When I was writing *Angel On Board*, I wrote it in secret for 3 years, with only one dear friend knowing what I was doing. My husband and his alcoholism were the antagonists of the story, so I had to keep the secret pretty close to the vest if I wanted to complete it.

When I was picking out names for the characters, I would basically let the characters pick out their own names. I focused on the character I was going to name, and if someone else's picture came into my head, I honored that person and named the character for them. My great-aunt Pearl for example, was the name for Jeannie's guardian angel. When I focused on the main character, a strong African-American preacher, I saw the face of Martin Luther King and that character was named Martin.

Some of the names were a little harder to come up with and I had to look for inspiration. For instance, the character of the baby's father, I didn't really want to name him after someone I cared about because the character was basically a jerk through most of the book. And he had to have a signature' name. The name had to be close to a common name, but with a twist, just so he could hold a grudge if anyone ever called him by the more common pronunciation. I picked up the bible and opened straight to the book of Jeremiah. It was perfect, close enough to Jeremy, that with a little twist I could make it into JeremI—emphasis on the "I" at the end. That was the perfect name!

For Martin's last name, I couldn't think of anything, so I went over to the book case, and with my eyes closed, picked a book. I don't remember the name of the book, but it was printed by Harper & Row. Harper—what a perfect surname for angel!

So then, when I needed the name for the baby, it had to be an anagram using the names Martin and Sheila because that is how we really named our real baby by using the names of our dearly departeds and mixing up the letters. And I came up with a name -Marshal. I wasn't so sure about that one and it bothered me. I kept trying to rearrange the letters and couldn't come up with anything better, but I still wasn't convinced that Marshal was the right name. I decided that if I got some type of sign, I'd use it or change it depending on the message.

That year, we were planning a trip to Portland to watch the Rose Festival Parade. My husband had some family there and we went for the holiday weekend. As we were sitting down on the curb to pick our seats for the parade, my husband's aunt saw someone she knew and motioned for me to join her to greet them.

"EJ, I want you to meet Marshal, his son Marshal and his grandson Marshal," she smiled.

Again, this book was a secret and she had no idea that I had a character-naming dilemma on my mind, but the dilemma was solved in that very second! Confirmed not once, not twice, but three times! The baby in the book was going to be named Marshal!

Computer with a Mind of Its Own

by John Craig

A few months after my wife Jeanie passed away, a very strange event happened with her computer. I had left her desktop computer on her desk, in the corner of our bedroom, ever since she had last worked on her collection of stories about women in Yellowstone and the first few chapters of her fiction romance novel. All those files, and more, were still on that computer, but I kept putting off retrieving them, knowing full well I'd need to summon a lot of emotional strength to see what she had written in those files. "Soon," I told myself, "I'll get to that soon."

Now I know computers very well. I've authored multiple books on computer programming for Microsoft and other publishers, and I've programmed computers to control and monitor several of the world's largest solar energy fields. What happened to Jeanie's computer that evening has never ever happened before or since in all my experiences, and I can only conclude the event was way beyond normal explanation. Here's what happened.

One evening, I was laying on the big king-sized bed, chatting on the phone with EJ, my new fiance. EJ was a good friend of both myself and Jeanie before she passed. We were chatting about Jeanie, when suddenly the computer in the corner powered up all by itself. Of course, being a rational, scientific kind of person I immediately started analyzing the situation to figure out how in the world that computer had turned itself on. It had been off for many weeks, nobody else was in the room with me, the lights in the room were on so there was no power surge, there were no dogs, cats, mice, bugs, kids ... I quickly ran out of ideas. Somehow, inexplicably, that computer had suddenly powered up as though someone had flipped its power switch!

While still on the phone with EJ, I walked over to the computer and immediately noticed on its desktop some Word documents. Opening them up one by one, I discovered several stories and writings that Jeanie had not told me about. They were wonderful. As I spent some time reading through them, I had the strongest feeling that Jeanie was there, sharing with me, looking over my shoulder as I read. My emotions ran the full range, from sheer joy at this unexpected communication, balanced with intense pangs of grief that I knew were therapeutic but nevertheless painful.

EJ is a publisher, so over the next few weeks we pulled together content from Jeanie's files to publish a small book for family members. Jeanie had a strong, loving personality, and it didn't surprise me in the least that she found a way to share her writings with us all. I'm convinced that having that computer wake up like it did was her way of giving me a wake up call to get her writings shared.

What a nice gift for us all - something we'll all cherish for a long time.

Birds & other Winged Creatures

Angels around us, angels beside us,
angels within us. Angels are watching over
you when times are good or stressed.
Their wings wrap gently around you,
whispering you are loved and blessed.

- Blessing

Funeral Birds

by EJ Thornton

My sister-in-law Jan passed away suddenly when she was 39. She was well-loved and it was standing-room-only at her funeral. Jan was a beautiful soul and loved with her whole heart. And her family believed in miracles.

During the procession to the cemetery, there was a bird, a seagull most likely, but a white bird leading the procession. We were back in the line about 10-15 cars and it was clear the bird was staying with the cars exactly. That was cool, and we were driving in a straight line, so it was easy to believe the bird would just fly away at the first turn.

However, it made the turn first, then the cars followed. The bird was showing them the way. It stayed with the procession for three turns and flew away when the procession finally reached the cemetery.

We knew it was a sign from Jan that she was still nearby.

I was telling Jan's funeral bird' story to my kids after the memorial service for my mother Connie who died in 2009 after a long bout with COPD.

My mom had a long-standing history with birds, not a very good one at that. The most memorable one—and one that shaped her disdain for birds was the one when she was a 12-year-old girl. She was given a freshly-killed duck and told to get it ready for dinner. She had no idea how to do it, but she did her best all the same because she had no choice. It was a horrible task to ask a young girl, but those were the times she lived in and the family situation she had to endure. She did her best to clean and dress the duck, and she put it in the baking dish and put it in the oven. The duck started to quack. It was distressing and horrible sound, spooky as well. Her father, who never ever wasted food, took the duck from the oven and threw it away. No one in their family could have eaten that duck.

Because of that story, I told my kids that I'd really be surprised if we had any birds show us the way to her graveside service. I was right, we got there and sat down -without incident.

My uncle, her brother was the presiding pastor. Everyone was present and he was just about to open his mouth to say, "We are gathered here today..." when a huge flock of geese took off and flew overhead honking the whole way. For most of a minute the honking was so loud no one could hear anyone else speak, even if they were right next to them. It got comical. The mood was completely lightened, still reverent, but the graveside service was more light-hearted than any of us imagined because all the sadness was lifted off by a fun flock of geese.

The Woman at the Well

by Grace Russell

I had been a pilot all my life and that's something to say, because not too many women were pilots in the 40's and 50's, but I was! I lead an interesting life from humble beginnings on an Indian reservation.

We grew up poor as most everyone did there, and my mom dressed me in an old flour sack she'd altered to be a dress. One day I was walking across a field in the wind and my dress fluttered around me. My mother thought it looked like it gave me wings and she gifted me my Indian name after that "Little White Dove."

Fast-forward a few years to 1979, like about 60 and I decided I'd done enough traveling and was ready to settle down. I found a nice farmhouse near Brighton, Colorado and it had a well that flowed delicious water.

The water was so good, that neighbors came from miles around to fill up with it. They offered to pay me, so I took 25 cents per gallon. I didn't know that this was going to get me in hot water with the state. Selling water made me a commercial well.' The state demanded that I drill a new well and have the water tested scientifically.

My friends and neighbors promised that they'd still buy my water if I took the big step of drilling a commercial well. The main concern was that my well was so deep (about 680 feet or more), that it was going to be dreadfully expensive. We took the plunge and decided to do it.

My well water was tested and it was found to be so pure that I'm the only commercial well in the state of Colorado that doesn't have to put any chemicals in the water to get it pure enough to drink. It pumps ancient and pure water from deep down under the surface water table from an ancient river bed.

I called it "The Fountain of Health" and I still own and operate it today with my husband Bud.

I knew the water was pure and I wanted it to stay that way, so I asked Father John to come and bless the well before we sold any of the water.

I bought a statue of St. Francis of Assissi and built an arch around him so that ivy could grow on it and it could act as a sacred space over the well.

During the ceremony, Father John gave a beautiful invocation and as he did, a little white dove flew over and sat right on the fence by me. He stayed there only long enough for me to notice him, and then he flew into a neighboring tree.

My Indian name was Little White Dove. This was such a special blessing, I could barely contain how amazing it made me feel. I cried, I laughed, I knew I was being blessed. I knew my well was too.

After Father John finished his blessing of the well, the white dove flew over to where we were and started to circle. Then it was joined by dozens and dozens of other white doves—where they came from, I do not know. The birds all circled higher and higher in the sky until I couldn't see them anymore.

I've always remembered that moment and the moment my mother named me Little White Dove and because of those two things, I always wear white. I know my water blesses people. It is pure and sweet and since there are no chemicals in it, my customers and friends let me know how much better they are feeling because they are drinking this pure and blessed water. I can't say it is miraculous, but it makes people feel fantastic.

I work to greet everyone who comes to my well with a smile and I'm always sending them on their way with a heart-felt "God bless you." I know God has blessed me!

If you live in Colorado, come by for some cool, clear water!

Peace at Last

Ever felt an angel's breath in the gentle breeze?
A teardrop in the falling rain?
Hear a whisper amongst the rustle of leaves?
Or been kissed by a lone snowflake?
Nature is an angel's favorite hiding place.

- Carrie Latet

Survivor's Guilt

by Anonymous

After *Angel On Board* was written, EJ gave a couple of advance copies to her friends at Christian Writers of Idaho—a group where she was a charter member. She asked them for their feedback and to ask their opinions on how to get it published. This was still 1998, not even a year yet since she finished writing it.

One such woman, whose identity we are protecting, due to her current marital state, was given the book and came back to give EJ some advice, but not before she told her a story.

She was living in California and she and her husband at the time owned a private jet that they would take trips on. She had planned to take a trip with her husband, but cancelled on him at the last minute. He still went, but sadly, the plane crashed and she was left a widow.

Second guessing all the decisions that led up to the crash, "What if she had gone, could she have prevented it?" The What-if questions dogged her to a point of absolute despair. And they had for the past 12 years.

This story surprised EJ because EJ had met this woman's husband and they as a couple seemed very happy. But he was her second husband and she had never admitted her survivor's guilt to him, and she had never tried to work it out in therapy either. She just kept beating herself up with the What-if's and why did God take him and not her.

As she read *Angel On Board*, the story of an abrupt death of a man and the family he left behind, she found eerie parallels. She felt herself sitting on the same furniture as the characters did and she could hear her husband tell her the same things that Martin said to Glory.

In one scene, Glory sat down in Martin's chair and breathed deep just to catch any lasting scent still remaining of her beloved. Martin, the late husband and now-angel came to her side and comforted her. EJ's friend said that it was at that exact moment, as she read the scene, that she had an epiphany. She finally understood why she lived and he didn't. She finally understood that his work was done, but her's was not and that is why she lived on.

"It was just that simple," she told EJ, "but therein lies the truth and my peace. I still have something important to do. I understand now and I can release the guilt I've felt for not dying alongside of him in that plane crash."

The Apology

Sparkle Phillips

excerpt from **Finding Your Soul Mate**

I was at a week-long business networking conference about 1000 miles away from home. It was designed to be very inspirational and emotional. I was in the middle of a significant personal transformation—becoming suddenly single after a long relationship and realizing what actually was at the core of my continual failures in my relationships with men. It went back to an incident in my childhood where my Grandfather had said something unloving to me.

The conference proved to be extremely emotional. On the Thursday of the conference, I realized that if my Grandmother Grace (his wife) was still alive, it would have been her 100th birthday. That just heightened my emotions more...

On Grandmas's birthday, I had a wonderfully emotional experience during a visualization of my future. It was such an extraordinary and vivid vision that I actually shared it with two other people psychically. That doesn't really matter to this story. However, it was an amazingly intense experience.

I remember every aspect of this visualization to this day and expect to remember it forever.

I told many people at the conference of the experience and that it took place on Grandma's 100th birthday. They all thought it was fascinating. There were some intuitives in attendance at the conference as well, they greeted my Grandmother as I walked by them in the hall as if she was visibly walking beside me for the rest of that week. That was a little freaky, but actually quite comforting.

On Sunday, during another hugely emotional event—the closing ceremony—they played the song "*Amazing Grace.*" The last time I had heard that song was at my Grandmother Grace's funeral a little over 5 years prior, so I broke down and bawled like a baby. My friends stood beside me and tried to hold me up, but I slid down against the wall and just sat down and experienced the song in my own world.

"Why are you here so strong, Grandma? I don't understand," I psychically pleaded for insight.

Then, in an instant, there was a blast across my consciousness and it was the spirit of Grandfather. "I'm here too," he said. "And I want to tell you how sorry I am for anything I ever said that hurt you. I'm so sorry I hurt you."

I was stunned. I was basically in shock. I hadn't had an experience like that before and I can't prove to anyone it ever happened, but whether anyone believes me or not, is irrelevant, because in that instant, I experienced something amazing instant forgiveness.

For all the men I had forgiven and wished well in a private ceremony to release the pain they had caused me in my life, I hadn't forgiven or released my grandfather for the initial incident that was the foundation of all the crap I drew into my life later. It hadn't occurred to me to add him to that list, but it was clear that I probably wasn't going to be able to move on with my life until I forgave him and released him and the painful feelings from that early moment in my life—ultimately taking full responsibility for myself.

Grandfather hadn't asked for forgiveness, he just apologized. This was probably the first time in my life when I would have accepted his apology, because I was finally consciously aware of what an apology from him would truly signify.

I got back up and finished out the ceremony in complete silence, because I couldn't speak without completely breaking down to tears. Even though I was surrounded by completely supportive friends, I needed to process this by myself. I just kept the experience to myself and contemplated the beautiful significance it had on my life.

Our Contributors

(alphabetically)

Connie Blake—1930-2009—Connie is an angel now too and her stories live on through her children, grandchildren and great-grandchildren.

Floyd Blake—1928- 2012—Floyd is with Connie and their son John now and his presence is sorely missed, although his loved ones can still feel him nearby.

Capri Brock—Capri is a graphic designer and works for Books To Believe In as the director of new projects. She is the co-compiler of *Angel On Board—Real Life Stories* . Find out more about Capri at DesignsByCapri.com.

Amy Collette—Amy is the author of The Gratitude Connection. Amy enjoys looking at the positive side of life and loving every minute of it. Find out more about Amy at TheGratitudeConnection.com.

John Clark Craig—John lost his wife Jeanie quite unexpectedly, however Jeanie's powerful personality is still making her presence known even in this plane. John is an author of dozens of technical books published by Microsoft, O'Reilly Media and Books To Believe In. Find out more about them at JohnClarkCraig.com.

Christine Grininger—Christine is the author of How to Conquer Cancer and is a survivor of cancer 4 times over. She is strongly connected to her spiritual side. To find out more about Christine, visit NewWayToTreatCancer.com.

Cathy Peterson—is an angel on Earth having taken care of NICU babies for most of her adult life. Cathy has amazing stories of survival, divine intervention and the sheer beauty of faith that conquers all fear.

Sparkle Phillips—is the author of Finding Your Soul Mate and its companion book Finding Your Fortune. Her stories are amazing as well. Find out more about Sparkle at GreatRelationshipBooks.com

Grace Russell—owns and operates "The Fountain of Health" an artesian spring near Brighton, Colorado. The waters that flow from that well are so pure that she is the only commercial well in the state of Colorado with a waiver against adding chemicals or treating the water in any way. It is just pure sweet cool water. Find out more at FountainOfHealth.cc.

Othniel J. Seiden—Otti is Colorado's most prolific author and has written dozens and dozens of books on both health-related, historical and spiritual topics. His books are fascinating and can be found at BoomerBookSeries.com

Sue Scudder—Sue is the author of The Voice Across the Veil and her skills as a medium are verified by anyone who speaks to her. Sue is also a musician and just plain beautiful spirit. Find out more about Sue at SpeakingWithTheSpirits.com.

EJ Thornton—EJ wrote *Angel On Board* in 1998 as a message to one man to quit using his grief as an excuse to stay drunk because that wasn't honoring those who had passed on. She had a vision of what those loved ones would want to say to him and so she wrote *Angel On Board*. The events surrounding *Angel On Board's* writing, publishing and release were as stunning as the angelic messages she's always received in her life. EJ lost her brother John when he was a young father and John's presence as well as the presence of both of her husband's angels have clearly influenced her life. Find out more about EJ at EJThornton.com.

Angel On Board— Real Life Stories

Now, it's your turn

Angel On Board—Real Life Stories, is a collection of readers' stories that are so extraordinary that the hand of the angels can clearly be seen. Some are about visions of angels, others about extraordinary people who were nothing short of angels, and others about miraculous events. If you have a "Real Life Story," please submit it for consideration:

Angel On Board—Real Life Stories
c/o Books To Believe In
17011 Lincoln Ave. #408
Parker, CO 80134

or submit it online via

GreatAngelBooks.com

Stories must be 2500 words or less and must represent a real event in your life and must include your bio.

31404154R00069

Printed in Poland
by Amazon Fulfillment
Poland Sp. z o.o., Wrocław